SEPTEMBER 2023

IN THE SHADOW OF SHADOW OF UKRAINE

RUSSIAN CONCEPTS OF FUTURE WAR AND FORCE DESIGN

Seth G. Jones

A REPORT OF THE CSIS TRANSNATIONAL THREATS PROJECT

CSIS | CENTER FOR STRATEGIC & INTERNATIONAL STUDIES

ROWMAN & LITTLEFIELD

Lanham · Boulder · New York · London

ABOUT CSIS

The Center for Strategic and International Studies (CSIS) is a bipartisan, nonprofit policy research organization dedicated to advancing practical ideas to address the world's greatest challenges.

Thomas J. Pritzker was named chairman of the CSIS Board of Trustees in 2015, succeeding former U.S. senator Sam Nunn (D-GA). Founded in 1962, CSIS is led by John J. Hamre, who has served as president and chief executive officer since 2000.

CSIS's purpose is to define the future of national security. We are guided by a distinct set of values—nonpartisanship, independent thought, innovative thinking, cross-disciplinary scholarship, integrity and professionalism, and talent development. CSIS's values work in concert toward the goal of making real-world impact.

CSIS scholars bring their policy expertise, judgment, and robust networks to their research, analysis, and recommendations. We organize conferences, publish, lecture, and make media appearances that aim to increase the knowledge, awareness, and salience of policy issues with relevant stakeholders and the interested public.

CSIS has impact when our research helps to inform the decisionmaking of key policymakers and the thinking of key influencers. We work toward a vision of a safer and more prosperous world.

CSIS does not take specific policy positions; accordingly, all views expressed herein should be understood to be solely those of the author(s).

© 2023 by the Center for Strategic and International Studies. All rights reserved.

ISBN: 978-1-5381-7072-4 (pb); 978-1-5381-7073-1 (eBook)

Center for Strategic & International Studies
1616 Rhode Island Avenue, NW
Washington, DC 20036
202-887-0200 | www.csis.org

Rowman & Littlefield
4501 Forbes Boulevard
Lanham, MD 20706
301-459-3366 | www.rowman.com

ACKNOWLEDGMENTS

This report was a team effort. A wide range of individuals were critical during the research, writing, and production phases of this project. Riley McCabe was extremely helpful at all stages of this report, from providing research assistance to helping move the manuscript through the publications process. Delaney Duff was invaluable in providing research assistance, including on Russian documents. The author is also grateful to Mark Cancian, Daniel Byman, and Alexander Palmer for their thorough reviews of an early draft. Their comments, critiques, and suggestions were extraordinarily helpful in improving the quality of this report. Thanks also to a superb group of colleagues at CSIS whose work on Europe and defense-related issues contributed to this report. They include Max Bergmann, Eliot Cohen, Cynthia Cook, Dan Fata, John Hamre, Kathleen McInnis, Sean Monaghan, and Maria Snegovaya. The author also greatly benefitted from conversations with several individuals along the way, including Dima Adamsky, General (ret.) Michael Hayden, Dara Massicot, Phillips O'Brien, General (ret.) David Petraeus, Michael Rouland, Philip Wasielewski, and Admiral (ret.) Sandy Winnefeld.

Thanks to CSIS's outstanding iLab team for their help in editing, formatting, and publishing the document. They include Lauren Adler, Lauren Bailey, Emma Colbran, Alex Kisling, Jeeah Lee, Phillip Meylan, Rayna Salam, and Katherine Stark.

Finally, thanks to those government officials and subject matter experts from the United States, Finland, the United Kingdom, Estonia, Poland, Canada, France, Germany, Ukraine, and the North Atlantic Treaty Organization that the author interviewed over the course of this project. Most of them did not want to be identified by name, but this report could not have been done without their comments and practical, real-world knowledge.

This publication was funded by the Russia Strategic Initiative, U.S. European Command. The views expressed in this publication do not necessarily represent the views of the Department of Defense or the United States government.

"Each war has to be matched with a special strategic behavior; each war constitutes a particular case that requires establishing its own special logic instead of applying some template."[1]

— A.A. Svechin

CONTENTS

Executive Summary	1
Chapter 1: Introduction	4
Chapter 2: The Historical Context	6
Chapter 3: The Future of Warfare and Russian Force Design	11
Chapter 4: Conclusion	22
About the Author	27
Endnotes	28

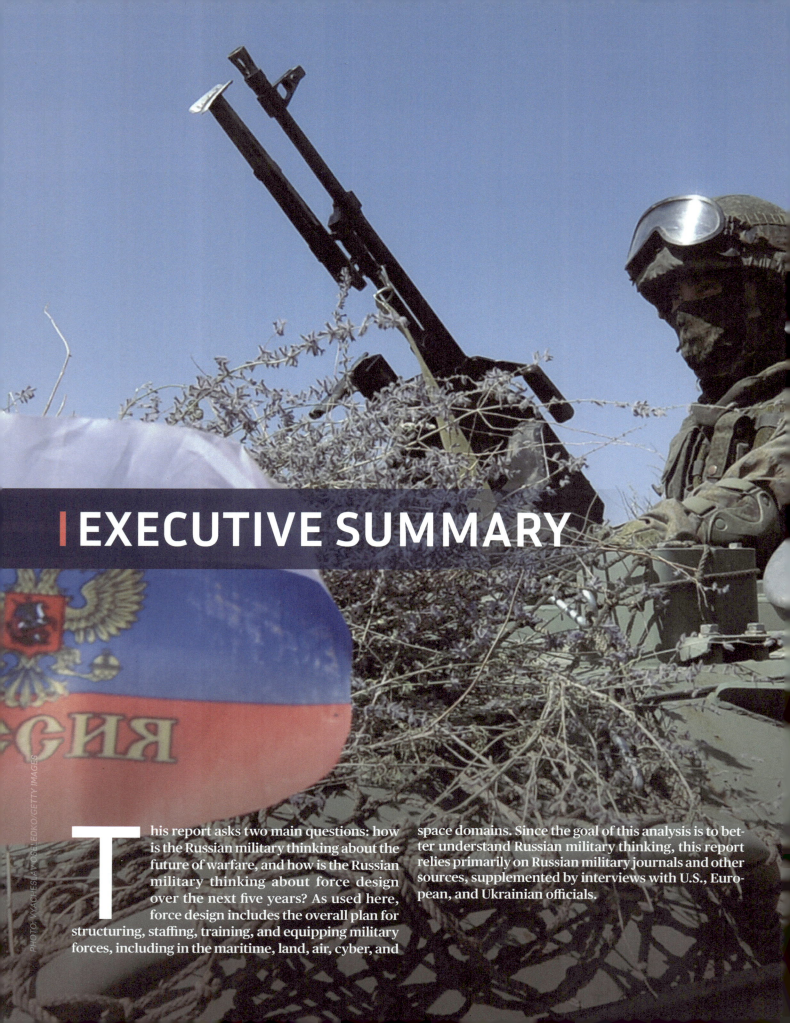

EXECUTIVE SUMMARY

This report asks two main questions: how is the Russian military thinking about the future of warfare, and how is the Russian military thinking about force design over the next five years? As used here, force design includes the overall plan for structuring, staffing, training, and equipping military forces, including in the maritime, land, air, cyber, and space domains. Since the goal of this analysis is to better understand Russian military thinking, this report relies primarily on Russian military journals and other sources, supplemented by interviews with U.S., European, and Ukrainian officials.

The report has several findings.

First, Russian military thinking is dominated by a view that the United States is—and will remain—Moscow's main enemy (главный враг) for the foreseeable future. This view of the United States as the main enemy has increased since the 2022 invasion, with significant implications for the future of warfare and force design. Russian political and military leaders assess that Russian struggles in Ukraine have been largely due to aid from the United States and North Atlantic Treaty Organization (NATO), which Russian leaders interpret as direct participation in the war. In addition, Russian leaders believe that the United States is attempting to expand its power, further encircle Russia, and weaken Russia militarily, politically, and economically. These sentiments make Russia a dangerous enemy over the next five years and will likely drive Moscow's desire to reconstitute its military as rapidly as possible, strengthen nuclear and conventional deterrence, prepare to fight the West if deterrence fails as part of a strategy of "active defense" (активная оборона), and engage in irregular and hybrid activities.

Second, Russian analyses generally conclude that while the *nature* of warfare—its essence and purpose—is unchanging, the *character* of future warfare will rapidly evolve in ways that require adaptation. This report focuses on four categories of interest to Russia: long-range, high-precision weapons; autonomous and unmanned systems; emerging technologies; and the utility of hybrid and irregular warfare. In these and other areas, Russian leaders assess that it will be critical to cooperate with other countries, such as China and Iran.

Third, Russian political and military leaders are committed to a major reconstitution of the Russian military—especially the Russian army—over the next several years, though achieving this goal will be challenging. Force design may evolve in the following areas:

- **Land**: Russian force design in land warfare will likely include an attempt to reconstitute the Russian army over the next five years. In particular, the army will likely continue to shift to a division structure, though it is unclear whether Russia can fill the ranks of larger units. These changes are a sharp divergence from the changes implemented under former minister of defense Anatoly Serdyukov. In addition, the Russian military has indicated a desire to restructure the army to allow for more mobility and decentralization in the field in response to the United States' and NATO's long-range precision strike capabilities.

- **Air**: Force design in the air domain will likely involve some reversals initiated by Serdyukov, as well as a major focus on unmanned aircraft systems (UASs). For example, the Russian military wants to increase the size of the Russian Aerospace Forces beyond the current force structure. Future developments may also include the use of UASs for logistics in contested environments, which will require new organizational structures.

- **Maritime**: The Russian military has expressed a desire to expand its naval forces in response to growing tensions with the United States and NATO. The Russian Ministry of Defense has outlined the creation of five naval infantry divisions for the navy's coastal troops. In addition, the Russian navy will likely increase the presence of unmanned maritime vessels as part of force design and focus on the development, production, and use of submarines.

- **Space and Cyber**: The Russian military will attempt to further develop its space and cyber capabilities, including offensive capabilities. It will also likely attempt to expand the size and activities of Russian Space Forces and a range of Russian cyber organizations, such as the Main Directorate of the General Staff (GRU), Foreign Intelligence Service (SVR), and Federal Security Service (FSB), though it will likely struggle in such areas as space because of Western sanctions.

Russia retains a significant arsenal of nuclear weapons, a relatively strong navy and air force that remain largely intact, and a reasonably good relationship with China and other countries, such as Iran, that could provide a much-needed jump start.

Nevertheless, Russia faces a suite of financial, military, political, social, and other issues that will force political and military leaders to *prioritize* changes in force design. Building a bigger navy and air force will be expensive, as will increasing the size of Russian ground forces. While it is impossible to predict with certainty how Russian leaders will prioritize force design changes, likely candidates are ones that are relatively cheap or essential to improve fighting effectiveness.

In the land domain, for example, the Russian army may prioritize restructuring its land forces around divisions, strengthening its defense industrial base to develop and produce precision munitions and weapons systems for a protracted war, and experimenting with tactical units to allow for greater mobility and autonomy against adversaries that have precision strike capabilities. Russia will likely rely on such countries as China, Iran, and North Korea for some weapons systems and components.

However, a successful reconstitution of the military and a redesign of the force, especially the army, will be difficult for several reasons.

First, Russia's deepening economic crisis will likely constrain its efforts to expand the quantity and quality of its ground, air, and naval forces. The war in Ukraine has fueled Russia's worst labor crunch in decades, and the Russian economy has been stressed by low growth, a decrease in the ruble against the dollar, and inflation. Second, corruption and graft remain rampant in the Russian military, which could undermine Moscow's overall plan to effectively structure, staff, train, and equip its forces. Third, Russia's defense industrial base will likely face challenges because of the war in Ukraine. Russia has already expended significant amounts of precision-guided and other munitions in the Ukraine war, and many of its weapons systems and equipment have been destroyed or severely worn down. Economic sanctions may create shortages of higher-end foreign components and force Moscow to substitute them with lower-quality alternatives. Fourth, Russia could face a significant challenge because of growing civil-military friction. Tension between the Russian military and population could worsen over time because of a protracted war in Ukraine, a languishing economy, and an increasingly authoritarian state. A reconstitution of the Russian military will likely require some level of support and sacrifice from the Russian population.

1 | INTRODUCTION

The Russian military has faced a wide range of shortcomings following its February 2022 invasion of Ukraine. Examples include a failure to conduct effective joint and combined arms operations, low morale of soldiers, inadequate leadership, poor logistics support to combat forces, and erroneous intelligence analyses. These problems have occurred despite considerable efforts by the Russian military to examine the future of war and to design a force capable of conducting effective conventional and hybrid operations. Russia's challenges in Ukraine have also severely undermined its security position. Finland and Sweden have opted to join the North Atlantic Treaty Organization (NATO), the West has imposed economic sanctions against Russia (including its defense industry), and the United States and other Western countries have provided significant military, economic, and political support to Ukraine.

These challenges have enormous implications for the future of the Russian military in an increasingly competitive security environment. After all, if the Russian military has struggled against Ukraine, how might Russia fare in a future war with the United States and other NATO countries?

RESEARCH DESIGN

To better understand Russian military thinking, this report asks two sets of questions. First, how is the Russian military thinking about the future of warfare? Second, how might the Russian military evolve its force design over the next five years? As used here, "force design" includes the overall plan for structuring, staffing, training, and equipping military forces, including maritime, land, and air forces. Force design directly affects manpower policies and retention goals. It also impacts "force structure," which includes the number and type of combat units a military can sustain, the forces a military has available, how they are equipped, and how they are organized.[1]

To answer the main questions, this report uses a mixed-methods approach. First, the research involved a compilation and translation of primary- and secondary-source Russian analyses of warfare and force design across multiple domains of war. Examples included Военная Мысль [*Military Thought*] and Вестник Академии Военных Наук [*Journal of the Academy of Military Sciences*]. A limited number of analytical opinion and commentary in such publications as Военно-промышленный курьер [*Military-Industrial Courier*], Красная звезда [*Red Star*], TASS, and others were also included.

While reviewing these documents is important, there are some limitations. For example, the quality of Russian military journals has declined over time—especially following the Russian invasion of Ukraine. Articles frequently lack innovative thought. Part of the reason may be because Russian military thinkers have few incentives to write critical and reflective pieces during a war that has gone poorly for the Russian military and in a country that has become increasingly totalitarian and wary of any criticism—explicit or implicit. In addition, this analysis uses only unclassified material. An assessment on Russian military thinking with access to classified information and analysis would still face information hurdles and gaps in knowledge. But a reliance on open-source information presents even greater hurdles. Nevertheless, taking precautionary steps—such as qualifying judgments where appropriate and identifying gaps in information—still leads to a useful understanding of Russian thinking on the future of warfare and force design.

Second, this report benefited from interviews with numerous government and subject matter experts. One example was a trip to NATO's eastern flank—including Finland, the Baltics, and Poland—to talk with military, political, and intelligence officials about how Russian military leaders view the future of warfare and force design. The report also benefited from interviews with officials from the United Kingdom, Germany, France, Canada, the United States, Ukraine, Finland, Estonia, Poland, and NATO, as well as discussions with a range of subject matter experts from such organizations as the Polish Institute of International Affairs, the Finnish Institute of International Affairs, and the International Institute for Strategic Studies.

ORGANIZATION OF THE REPORT

The rest of this report is divided into the following chapters. Chapter 2 examines the historical evolution of Russian thinking about the future of warfare and force design. Chapter 3 analyzes contemporary Russian thinking about the future of warfare and force design. Chapter 4 provides an overview of challenges that the Russian military may face in implementing these changes.

2 | THE HISTORICAL CONTEXT

This chapter briefly examines the evolution of Russian views on warfare and force design from the end of the Cold War to Russia's invasion of Ukraine in February 2022. It is not meant to be a comprehensive examination of historical trends in Russian views on warfare and force design, but rather is intended to establish a baseline for analyzing Russia today. Consequently, it focuses on three developments that are representative of the evolution of Russian military thinking on future warfare: precision weapons and related concepts, such as the reconnaissance-strike complex and reconnaissance-fire complex; force design, including the creation of battalion tactical groups (BTGs); and irregular and hybrid warfare.

The rest of this chapter is divided into four sections. The first examines the evolution in Russian thinking about precision weapons and related developments. The second section outlines the evolution of Russian force design. The third assesses Russian thinking about hybrid and irregular warfare. The fourth section provides a brief conclusion.

PRECISION WEAPONS

Beginning in the 1970s, Soviet military thinkers were at the forefront of grappling with the implications of technological innovations on warfare, what some called the Military-Technical Revolution (MTR).[1] One of the most influential figures was Marshal Nikolai Ogarkov, chief of the General Staff of the Soviet Union. According to Ogarkov, emerging technologies made it possible to see and strike deep in the future battlefield.[2] These advances required organizational and conceptual changes to adjust force design and structure in each military service.

Among the most significant advances were long-range, high-precision weapons, which could increase the potential for attacking an adversary's command-and-control facilities and lead to a compressed sensor-to-shooter kill chain. By the 1980s, the debate about the impact of the MTR led to the development of several concepts: deep operations battle, the reconnaissance-strike and reconnaissance-fire complexes; and operational maneuver groups.[3] In a 1983 article in *Red Star*, Ogarkov concluded that there were significant changes afoot in warfare because of "precision weapons, reconnaissance-strike complexes, and weapons based on new physical principles."[4] In a 1984 interview with *Red Star*, he noted that "the development of conventional means of destruction . . . is making many kinds of weapons global" and is triggering a rise "in the destructive potential of conventional weapons, making them almost as effective as weapons of mass destruction."[5]

After the end of the Cold War, Russian views on the future of warfare and force design were significantly impacted by a close examination of U.S. wars in Afghanistan, Iraq, Libya, the Balkans, and other areas, as well as Moscow's own experience in Chechnya, Georgia, Syria, and Ukraine. Russian military thinkers paid close attention to U.S. military operations and strategic thinking. The First Gulf War (1990-1991) and Second Gulf War (2003) were, in many ways, watershed moments for the Russian military. According to Russian analyses, the United States' technological superiority over the Iraqi military overwhelmed the numerical advantages of the Iraqi military. As one assessment concluded, "Reconnaissance, fire, electronic, and information warfare forces of different branches and arms of the service were integrated the first time ever into a shared spatially distributed reconnaissance and strike system making wide use of modern information technologies and automated troops and weapons control systems."[6]

The U.S. military began with a massive attack by some of the latest electronic warfare capabilities and then launched, in parallel, an offensive by the U.S. Air Force and sea-based cruise missiles, reinforced with reconnaissance strike aircraft and artillery barrages.[7]

In these operations, the U.S. military effectively used technologies to conduct non-contact warfare (бесконтактная война) in which much of the fighting would take place using stand-off precision weapons.[8] Medium- and long-range strikes from air, maritime, land, cyber, and even space-based platforms aided ground forces. As Major General Vladimir Slipchenko argued, for example, new technologies increased the importance of precision-guided weapons (or высокоточное оружие) and increased the role of airpower and the information components of war (including psychological operations, electronic warfare, and cyber warfare).[9] The origins of Russian approaches toward non-contact warfare stem, in part, from the leading Russian military theorists inspired by the intellectual legacy of Ogarkov's revolution in military affairs.[10]

Integrating these technologies into warfare would also require an evolution in concepts. One of the most important was an evolution in the reconnaissance strike complex (or разведывательно-ударный комплекс) for stand-off strike, which involved the need to collect real-time intelligence and quickly push information to air, ground, and maritime units for strikes.[11] A major goal of the reconnaissance strike complex was to improve command, control, communications, computers, intelligence, surveillance, and reconnaissance (C4ISR) on the battlefield to facilitate the coordinated employment of high-precision, long-range weapons linked to real-time intelligence data.

Russian operations in Syria underscored the growing importance of precision strike to support ground force advances and to hit adversary logistics hubs and other targets. A growing reliance on long-range strike requires sufficient stockpiles of munitions (especially precision-guided munitions); an arms production capacity able to produce munitions in sufficient quantities; adequate intelligence, surveillance, and reconnaissance (ISR) capabilities to identify potential targets; and an all-domain command-and-control system that allows users to quickly take advantage of real-time intelligence.

Russia integrated its air operations into a reconnaissance-strike complex. The Russian military heavily relied on medium-range and long-range strike from air, land, and maritime platforms and systems to help ground forces take–and retake–territory. Moscow combined air operations with ground-based fires and sea-launched stand-off weapons.[12] At the tactical level, Russia attempted to establish kill chains that flowed from sensors to warfighters.[13] In addition, Russia took advantage of the relatively permissive environment in Syria to test and refine this concept, integrating strikes from fixed-wing aircraft with unmanned aircraft systems (UASs), such as the Orlan-10, Forpost, and Eleron-3SV; electronic warfare; space-based systems; and other ISR platforms and systems.[14]

However, there were challenges with the reconnaissance-strike complex. To begin with, Russia lacked sufficient numbers of pre-

A Forpost from Russia's Baltic Fleet flies overhead in the Kaliningrad region.

Russian Ministry of Defense.

cision-guided munitions. Roughly 80 percent of ordnance dropped over the first few months of the war in Syria were unguided bombs from Su-24s and Su-25s.[15] In addition, the only dedicated airborne ISR assets that the Russian air force maintained in Syria were a small number of IL-20 Coots and the intermittent presence of a Tu-214R ISR testbed aircraft. The Russian air group's pool of potential intelligence collectors was further thinned by a shortage of targeting pods that impaired the ability of Russian fighters to provide the kind of nontraditional ISR that Western militaries possess. The Russian air force could not match the 1:2 ISR-to-strike sortie ratio maintained by U.S. and coalition air forces in Iraq and Syria, much less the 4:1 ratio that NATO executed over Afghanistan.[16]

In addition, most Russian sorties in Syria were still deliberately planned missions. The Russian air force did not effectively operationalize the processes necessary to react on the fly to unexpected battlefield emergencies and was unable to take full advantage of its reconnaissance-strike complex. Russia failed to conduct the ground-directed dynamic targeting that has come to define most Western air operations.[17]

FORCE DESIGN

Based on the Russian military's views about the future of warfare, Russian force design evolved through the invasion of Ukraine in 2022. Russian thinkers based force design, in part, on a strategy of active defense (активная оборона).[18] The concept of a strong defense has a long and rich tradition in Russian military thinking, including from such individuals as Alexander Svechin.[19] It involved integrating preemptive measures and—if that failed—denying an opponent a decisive victory in the initial period of war by degrading their effort and setting the conditions for a counteroffensive. The strategy privileged a permanent standing force, arrayed as high-readiness operational formations in each strategic direction.[20]

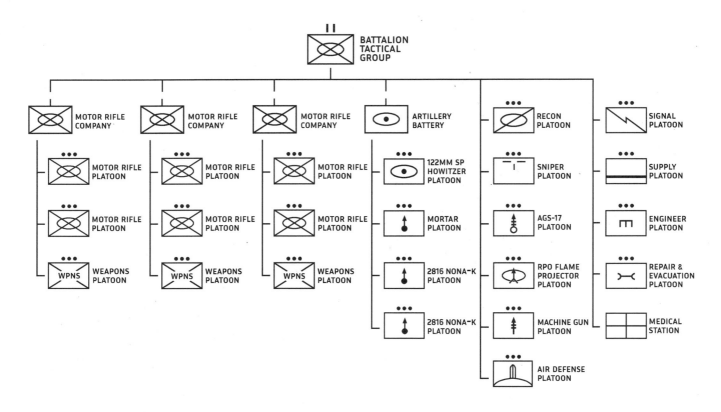

Figure 2.1: Example of a Russian Battalion Tactical Group.

Mark Galeotti, Armies of Russia's War in Ukraine (New York: Osprey, 2019), 40; and Dmanrock29, "Russian Battalion Tactical Group," Wikimedia Commons (CC BY-SA 4.0).

One important period in force design was defense minister Anatoly Serdyukov's "New Look" reform beginning in 2008, which led to one of the most radical changes in the Russian military since World War II.[21] The goal was to create a flexible, professional army in a permanent combat-ready state that was able to mount a spectrum of operations from small-scale interventions to high-end warfare. Serdyukov reduced the size of the armed forces from 1.13 million to 1 million by 2012, and he decreased the size of the officer corps as well. As Serdyukov put it, "our army today is reminiscent of an egg which is swollen in the middle. There are more colonels and lieutenant colonels than there are junior officers."[22] Overall, the division gave way to a smaller, more flexible structure at the battalion level.

The reforms led to the dismissal of 200 generals, and the military cut nearly 205,000 officer positions. Before the reforms, the Russian order of battle resembled a smaller Soviet one, with 24 divisions, 12 independent brigades, and two separate external task forces deployed to Armenia and Tajikistan. However, only six divisions—five motor rifle divisions and a tank division—were at full strength and operational.[23] Russian leaders believed that a smaller but better-equipped and -trained military could handle a range of conflicts. This process took place largely between 2008 and 2012.[24] The army's fighting force comprised 4 tank brigades, 35 motor rifle brigades and a cover, or fortification, brigade, supported by 9 missile, 9 artillery, 4 Multiple Launch Rocket Systems, 9 air defense, and 10 support brigades. This left the army with 85 brigades, 40 of which were frontline combat units.[25]

Around 2015, however, the Russian military partially revived larger formations geared for major wars. In 2016, the military reactivated the First Tank Army in the Western Military District, including two reestablished divisions of long and revered history: the 4th Guards Kantemirovskaya Tank Division and a reformed 2nd Guards Tamanskaya Motorized Rifle Division that had been the first converted to a brigade.[26]

The Russian military eventually adopted a force structure that could deploy as BTGs, or as the entire formation, such as a regiment or brigade. BTGs were combined arms units, which were typically drawn from all-volunteer companies and battalions in existing brigades. They were task-organized motorized rifle or tank combat entities designed to perform semi-independent combined arms operations. The goal was for Russians to deploy meaningfully sized field forces drawn from "kontraktniki" (or контрактники)–professionals who were better trained than conscripts and legally deployable abroad. While the structure of the BTGs varied somewhat based on operational needs and available personnel, most included roughly 600 to 800 soldiers. As highlighted in Figure 2.1, they were generally mechanized battalions, with two to four tank or mechanized infantry companies and attached artillery, reconnaissance, engineer, electronic warfare, and rear support platoons. The support platoon generally consisted of motor transport, field mess, vehicle recovery, maintenance, and hygiene squads. The result was a somewhat self-sufficient ground combat unit with disproportionate fire and rear support.[27] Most BTGs had sufficient ammunition, food, and fuel in high-intensity combat for one to three days before needing logistics support.[28]

HYBRID WARFARE

Finally, Russia relied on a mix of regular and irregular actions– or hybrid warfare (гибридная война). As used here, irregular warfare refers to activities short of regular (or conventional) warfare that are designed to expand a country's influence and weaken its adversaries. Examples include information and disinformation operations, cyber operations, support to state and non-state partners, covert action, espionage, and economic coercion.[29] In addition, hybrid warfare involves the combination of regular and irregular warfare.[30]

State and non-state partner forces played a critical role in conducting ground operations—including fire and maneuver—with outside training, advising, and assistance efforts. In Syria, for example, Russia benefited from competent and well-trained Lebanese Hezbollah forces, which were well equipped and had significant experience fighting highly capable Israel Defense Force units in 2006 in Lebanon. Hezbollah forces were tactically and operationally proficient at cover and concealment, fire discipline, mortar marksmanship, and coordination of direct-fire support, which were helpful for their involvement in the Syrian war.[31] Moscow also worked with militias whose members were recruited from Iraq, Palestinian territory, Syria, Afghanistan, Pakistan, and other locations.

Russia also leveraged private military companies (PMCs), such as the Wagner Group, which trained and advised Syrian army units and a number of pro-Assad and foreign militias fighting for the regime, including the 5th Corps and Shia militias such as the Palestinian Liwa al-Quds.[32] PMCs provided training to other Russian-backed Syrian militias, such as Sayadou Da'esh (Islamic State Hunters), which emerged in early 2017 and was deployed to protect installations in and around Palmyra, including the military airport and oil and gas fields. Other Russian PMCs, such as Vegacy Strategic Services, conducted smaller training missions for pro-regime militia forces, such as Liwa al-Quds.[33] In addition, PMCs engaged in some urban clearing operations. Wagner Group forces, for example, participated in operations at Latakia, Aleppo, Homs, Hama, and greater Damascus, as well as the counteroffensive to retake Palmyra in 2016 and 2017.[34]

More broadly, Moscow expanded its overseas use of PMCs to over two dozen countries, such as Ukraine, Libya, Sudan, Mali, the Central African Republic, Mozambique, and Venezuela. These countries spanned Africa, the Middle East, Europe, Asia, and Latin America. Russian PMCs cooperated closely with the Russian government, including various combinations of the Kremlin, Ministry of Defense, Foreign Intelligence Service, and Federal Security Service. PMCs performed a variety of tasks, such as combat operations, intelligence collection and analysis, protective services, training, site security, information operations, and propaganda to further Moscow's interests.[35]

CONCLUSION

By Russia's February 2022 invasion of Ukraine, the military had become a partial-mobilization force. Its leaders hoped to have more forces and equipment, reduced staffing and costs, and the ability to generate substantial combat power on short notice. The Russian military had also shed much of its Soviet legacy. It was ostensibly well suited to short, high-intensity campaigns defined by a heavy use of artillery and precision weapons, bolstered by such concepts as the reconnaissance-strike complex and reconnaissance-fire complex. The military could also conduct hybrid warfare by combining regular and irregular operations. Russian leaders were bolstered by the military's success in helping the Bashar al-Assad government retake much of its territory in Syria. As would soon become clear, however, the Russian military was unprepared—at least initially—for a conventional war of attrition.

3 | THE FUTURE OF WARFARE AND RUSSIAN FORCE DESIGN

This chapter asks two questions: how is the Russian military thinking about the future of warfare, and how might the Russian military evolve its force design over the next five years? The chapter makes two main arguments based on a review of Russian documents, supplemented by interviews. First, Russian analyses generally conclude that while the *nature* of warfare—its essence and purpose—is unchanging, the *character* of future warfare is rapidly evolving in ways that may force Moscow to adapt more quickly. Of particular interest to Russian military thinkers is the continuing growth in precision weapons; autonomous and unmanned systems; specific emerging technologies, such as artificial intelligence (AI), stealth, and electronic warfare; and hybrid warfare.

Second, Russian political and military leaders are committed to a major reconstitution of the Russian military—especially the Russian army—over the next several years, making Russia a serious threat. Future force design will likely focus on deterring and—if deterrence fails—fighting the United States and NATO if necessary. According to Russian assessments, the Russian military is considering evolving force design in several areas:

- **Land**: Russian force design in land warfare will likely include a continuing shift to divisions, although it is unclear whether the army can sufficiently fill the ranks of larger units. These changes mark a major shift away from the changes implemented under former minister of defense Anatoly Serdyukov. In addition, Russia will likely attempt to restructure its forces to allow for more mobility and decentralization in the field in response to U.S. and NATO long-range precision strike capabilities.

- **Air**: Force design in the air domain will likely involve some reversals initiated by Serdyukov, as well as a major focus on unmanned aircraft systems (UASs). For example, the Russian military will likely attempt to increase the size of the Russian Aerospace Forces. The Russian military may also partially restructure its air forces to incorporate a significant increase in the use of UASs. Future developments may include the use of UASs for logistics in contested environments, which will require new organizational structures.

- **Maritime**: Russia may expand its naval forces in response to growing tensions with the United States and NATO. The Ministry of Defense has expressed an interest in creating five naval infantry divisions for the navy's coastal troops based on existing naval infantry brigades.

- **Space and Cyber**: The Russian military will continue to develop its offensive space and cyber capabilities, including its electronic warfare capabilities. It will also likely try to expand the size and activities of the Russian Space Forces and a range of Russian cyber organizations, such as the Main Directorate of the General Staff (GRU), Foreign Intelligence Service (SVR), and Federal Security Service (FSB). But Russia will likely face serious challenges in implementing some of these changes, especially to the Russian Space Forces, because of Western sanctions and other factors.

Russia will likely face significant challenges in making all—or even most—of these changes, as outlined in the next chapter. Consequently, Russia will need to *prioritize* which steps it takes, as discussed in the last section of this chapter.

The rest of this chapter is divided into three sections. The first examines Russia's current thinking about the future of warfare. The second section assesses Russian thinking about force design. The third focuses on how Russia may prioritize among force design options.

THE FUTURE OF WARFARE

Russian military thinking generally assumes that the character of warfare is rapidly evolving, though the nature of warfare remains a violent struggle between opponents.[1] If there were any doubts before, the war in Ukraine has been a stark reminder. "War," Carl von Clausewitz writes, "is an act of violence intended to compel our opponent to fulfill our will."[2] War is still nasty and brutish. By contrast, the character of warfare—including the conduct of warfare, the speed and complexity of tactical decisionmaking, and the technology and weapons systems that militaries use and need—is evolving. In particular, technology is advancing in such areas as robotics, sensors, AI, cyber, space, long-range precision strike, hypersonics, and advanced communications, command, and control. There will also be an overload of information available to military and intelligence personnel that will be collected by space-based, aerial, ground, surface, sub-surface, and cyber sensors.

Overall, there are several themes about the future of warfare in Russian military thinking: contact versus non-contact warfare, autonomous and unmanned systems, technological innovation, and hybrid warfare. These are not meant to be exhaustive, but rather representative of some of the most important themes debated by Russian military thinkers.

Contact vs. Non-Contact Warfare: There remains a tension in Russian military thinking between the future prevalence of contact warfare (контактная война) and non-contact warfare (бесконтактная война). On the one hand, numerous Russian military thinkers believe that warfare involving long-range precision weapons will become ubiquitous. On the other hand, many also believe that warfare will still involve violent contact between opposing ground forces that fight for control of territory. Russian military thinkers appear to be grappling with how to fight for control of territory while dealing with an adversary's long-range precision strike.

Russian military analysts generally agree that there will be a continuing development of advanced precision weapons that allow for a "high level of target destruction."[3] The goal of non-contact warfare is to destroy the adversary's will and ability to fight at a distance before any contact occurs—or, at the very least, to strike fixed-wing aircraft, air defense systems, and other targets and weaken the adversary's ability to hit back or defend itself. Conducting these types of attacks will increasingly require good intelligence about the adversary's locations, plans, and intentions.[4]

The importance of long-range air, ground, and naval fires in Ukraine has reinforced the need to continue developing precision capabilities and the reconnaissance-strike complex (разведывательно-ударный комплекс) and reconnaissance-fire complex (разведывательно-огневой комплекс).[5] After all, Russian forces have failed to conduct dynamic targeting in Ukraine and to quickly move from sensor to shooter in a kill chain. Ukraine has also demonstrated that long-range precision strike may require large volumes of munitions when facing an adversary with good—or reasonably good—air defense capabilities.[6]

Nevertheless, Ukraine has highlighted the persistence of contact warfare and the need to fight for control of physical territory. As one Russian analysis concludes, "There is no reason to expect that [long-range precision weapons] will render useless the more advanced forms and methods of contact warfare. . . . [T]he supporters of this theory spread false information, arguing that modern and, above all, future wars will only be non-contact."[7] Warfare will still hinge, in part, on the struggle for territorial control that involves the use of brute force among armies.[8]

The broader debate about contact and non-contact warfare has at least three implications. First, Russia and its partners (such as China) will be in a race with its adversaries (such as the United States) to develop precision weapons that are faster, stealthier, longer range, and carry a higher payload. Examples include the use of more advanced seekers, improved surface material on missiles, laser guidance, anti-jamming capabilities, sensors, and robust algorithms for precision strike. Second, the growth in precision weapons will present significant dangers to ground forces, which will be exposed to saturation from medium- and long-range strikes.[9] As discussed later in this chapter, ground forces will likely need to be more mobile and decentralized. Third, Russian assessments conclude that the military needs to expedite defensive measures to protect civilian and military targets. One area is integrated air and missile defense to defend against incoming stand-off weapons. Another is denial and deception (maskirovka, or маскировка) to make it more difficult for adversaries to identify and hit targets, including the use of concealment, thermal camouflage, anti-thermal material, imitation with decoys and dummies, denial, disinformation, and other tactics, techniques, and procedures.

Autonomous and Unmanned Systems: Russian assessments of the future of war assume a growing role for all types of unmanned systems—air, land, surface, and sub-surface.[10] The importance of unmanned systems also means that a key aspect of future warfare will be countering these systems.

UASs—including micro- and mini-UASs—offer a useful example of Russian thinking on unmanned systems. According to a range of Russian military analysis, UASs will be increasingly critical for future warfare because of their utility for aerial reconnaissance, target designation for artillery and other weapons systems, precision strike, attack assessment, survey of terrain to produce digital maps, logistics (such as moving cargo), aerial refueling, communications, and electronic warfare. While UASs were often utilized in the past for intelligence, surveillance, and reconnaissance (ISR) and strike operations, they will likely be important for combined arms operations in the future—including a critical part of Russia's reconnaissance-strike complex. As Russian president Vladimir Putin remarked:

> [T]he use of drones has become practically ubiquitous. They should be a must-have for combat units, platoons, companies and battalions. Targets must be identified as quickly as possible and information needed to strike must be transferred in real time. Unmanned vehicles should be interconnected, integrated into a single intelligence network, and should have secure communication channels with headquarters and commanders. In the near future, every fighter should be able to receive information transmitted from drones.[11]

Numerous countries—including the United States—are pouring research and development resources into autonomous and unmanned systems. As Russian analysts recognize, for example, the U.S. Department of Defense and defense industry are working on such unmanned systems as the collaborative combat aircraft (including the Gambit, X-62 Vista, and XQ-58 Valkyrie), MQ-28 Ghost Bat, MQ-25 Stingray, MQ-1C Gray Eagle Extended Range, and loitering munitions such as the Phoenix Ghost and Switchblade lines.[12] These efforts also include the development of AI so that unmanned systems can be entirely autonomous.

The Russian military is also working to develop future swarming tactics for UASs. A swarm involves a large number of drones flying in a coordinated fashion.[13] The integration of AI would allow UASs to make decisions on their own.[14] Swarms could be particularly beneficial for strike operations if UASs could independently search for—and destroy—targets and adapt quickly to evolving conditions.[15] Russia has watched with interest the swarming programs of adversaries, including the United States and United Kingdom.[16] Development efforts may focus on intensifying information exchange among UASs, reducing their dimensions, enhancing their maneuverability, and minimizing their construction costs.[17]

Russian assessments also conclude that the Russian military will need to improve its ability to counter unmanned systems.[18] While Russia needs to develop and produce unmanned systems, so will its state and non-state adversaries. UASs will increasingly proliferate to state and non-state actors because the barriers to acquisition are so low.[19] Many are inexpensive and commercially available. In addition, some Russian analysis suggests that advancements in engines, energy-saving technologies (such as high-energy solar arrays made from silicon, lithium, iron, and phosphate technologies), batteries, and

STRIKE	LASER	ELECTRONIC	MICROWAVE	ACOUSTIC
■ Airframe, load-carrying structure ■ Electronic assets ■ Engine ■ Fuel system ■ Optoelectronic system ■ Payload	■ Airframe, load-carrying structure ■ Electronic assets ■ Engine ■ Fuel system ■ Optoelectronic system ■ Payload	■ Electronic assets ■ Optoelectronic system	■ Electronic assets ■ Optoelectronic system	■ Electronic assets ■ Engine

Figure 3.1: Russian Assessments of Vulnerable UAS Components.

Г.А. Лопин, Г.И. Смирнов, И.Н. Ткачёв [G.A. Lopin, G.I. Smirnov, and I.N. Tkachov], "Развитие Средств Борьбы С Беспилотными Летательными Аппаратами" [Development of Assets to Counter Unmanned Vehicles], Военная мысль [Military Thought] 32, no. 2 (June 2023): 58–67.

lightweight material will increase the range, speed, and payload capacities of UASs.[20]

Russian assessments generally conclude that surface-to-air missiles and artillery are not cost effective against UASs. In addition, ground radar detection of micro- and mini-UASs will be difficult because UASs can hover for protracted periods and some types have a low Doppler frequency, making them difficult to detect.[21] As one Russian assessment concludes, "The use of drones at all levels of armed formations, as well as the range of missions they perform, will constantly expand. This trend is expected to continue in the coming years. Thus, a program for designing and developing specialized radars and weapons of the given and prospective classes of micro- and mini-UAVs needs to be adopted."[22]

Consequently, Russia is working on possible solutions that target critical subsystems of UASs using advanced electronic warfare systems, lasers, microwave weapons, and acoustic weapons. As Figure 3.1 highlights based on one Russian analysis, electronic warfare may be particularly useful against UAS electronic assets and optoelectronic systems, lasers against all key subsystems, microwaves against electronic assets and optoelectronic systems, acoustics against engines and electronic assets, and strike against all major subsystems. Electronic warfare appears to be especially promising for Russian military analysts.[23]

Russia has devoted research and development resources to examine various ways to counter UASs, such as installing miniature radars on UASs to double or triple the range for detecting incoming UASs.[24] As Figure 3.2 highlights, this could include UASs operating in threatened sectors, while transmitters on antenna masts illuminate the reconnaissance area from protected positions.

Emerging Technologies: Another major theme of Russian military thinking is the growing importance of emerging technologies. As Russian strategic thinkers recognize, the United States and other NATO countries are investing in significant technological innovations. The previous section highlighted one area: unmanned systems. This section examines several others that Russian military thinkers believe may be important for future warfare.

One emerging technology is the use of AI.[25] According to some Russian analyses, AI will lead to the emergence of new forms of offense and defense, such as swarms, autonomous unmanned systems, global cyber operations, and missile defense.[26] As one Russian assessment concludes, the future will likely include "the emergence of highly autonomous combat systems in all areas of armed struggle, the transition from individual tactical unit control (items of weapons, military, and specialized hardware) and tactical groups to control systems based on AI."[27] Russia is engaged in AI

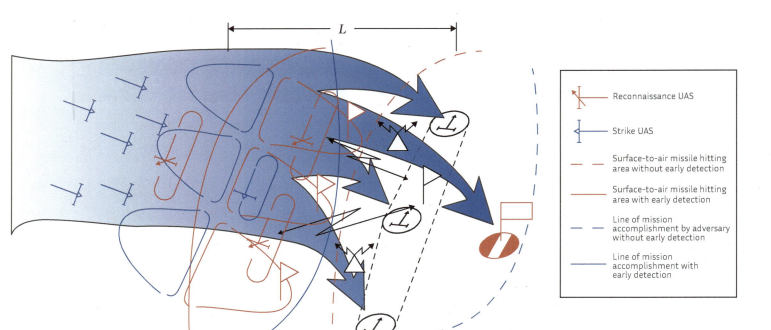

Figure 3.2: Russian Analysis of UASs to Counter Unmanned Systems.

Мариам Мохаммад, В. Н. Похващев, Л. Б. Рязанцев [Mariam Mohammad, V.N. Pokhvashchev, and L.B. Ryazantsev], "К Вопросу Повышения Эффективности Противодействия Малоразмерным Беспилотным Летательным Аппаратам" [Improving the Efficiency of Countering Small Unmanned Aerial Vehicles], Военная мысль [Military Thought] 31, no. 4 (December 2022), 71.

development in multiple areas, such as image identification, speech recognition, control of autonomous military systems, and information support for weapons.[28]

Another example is hypersonic technology.[29] Hypersonic weapons combine the speed and range of ballistic missiles with the low altitude and maneuverability profile of a cruise missile, making them difficult to detect and capable of quickly striking targets. As one Russian assessment concludes, future warfare will involve the "widespread proliferation of hypersonic weapons in the air environment and supersonic weapons in the marine environment."[30] The Russian military is particularly interested in hypersonic technology because hypersonic cruise and ballistic missiles can overcome an adversary's integrated air and missile defense and destroy its retaliatory strike systems.[31]

The Russian military is also interested in the future military application of other technologies, such as biotechnology, telecommunications, nanotechnology, quantum computing, stealth technology, laser weapons, and directed energy weapons.[32]

While this section highlights Russian *interest* in integrating emerging technology into its military, Russia is not a global leader in many of these technologies. Consequently, Moscow will likely lag behind such countries as the United States and China, which are pouring more money into the defense sector and have much greater capabilities. Russia has also suffered from a brain drain of talent in the technology sector. More founders of "unicorn" startups–privately held startup companies with a value of over $1 billion–leave Russia than any other country, according to one study.[33] Another assesses that the Russian tech sector is hemorrhaging and is in danger of being "cut off from the global tech industry, research funding, scientific exchanges, and critical components."[34]

Hybrid Warfare: Finally, Russian military thinkers assess that the future of warfare will include a combination of both state and non-state actors involved in regular and irregular operations, which may be best characterized as hybrid warfare.[35] The concept of hybrid warfare has a long and rich tradition in Russian military thinking. Over the past several years, Russia has used government forces (such as special operations forces and intelligence units) and non-government forces (such as private military companies and Lebanese Hezbollah) to conduct extraterritorial actions.[36] The Russian military may be cautious about leveraging some types of non-state or quasi-state actors in light of Yevgeny Prigozhin's tension with the Russian military and insurrection against the Russian government in June 2023. But hybrid warfare will likely remain important for the Russian state. In fact, Russia's challenges in conducting conventional warfare in Ukraine may *increase* Moscow's proclivity for hybrid warfare, especially against the United States and other NATO countries that have superior conventional capabilities.

According to Russian analyses, future warfare will continue to involve non-state actors.[37] After all, Russian analysts believe that such adversaries as the United States will utilize a wide range of non-state actors in the future to sow discord and instability.[38] Based on the Ukraine case, Russian analyses also assume that adversaries such as the United States will use Western companies in multiple domains of warfare, including cyber (such as Microsoft and Amazon) and space (such as SpaceX, Hawkeye 360, and Maxar).[39]

FORCE DESIGN

This section examines Russian thinking on force design, based in part on Russian assessments about the future of warfare. It focuses on several aspects of force design: land, air, maritime, cyber, and space. Chapter 4 then examines the challenges Moscow will likely face in implementing many of these changes.

Russian military thinking about force design is based on an assumption that the United States—and NATO more broadly—will be Russia's main enemy (главный враг) and greatest threat for the foreseeable future.[40] Russian leaders have expressed concern about the expansion of NATO to Finland and Sweden, as well as the buildup of Western forces—especially U.S. forces—on NATO's eastern flank.[41] In addition, Russian political and military leaders assess that Russia's struggles in Ukraine have been due to U.S. and broader NATO aid.[42]

Consequently, Russia has closely examined U.S. force design efforts, such as the U.S. Marine Corps' *Force Design 2030*.[43] *Force Design 2030* is in some ways an odd concept for Moscow to examine since it focuses on fighting a maritime conflict in the Indo-Pacific. But there are some broader discussions of the importance of precision fires and logistics in a contested environment. As *Force Design 2030* concludes, the future of the U.S. Marine Corps will center around such capabilities as:

▷ [L]ong-range precision fires; medium- to long-range air defense systems; short-range (point defense) air defense systems; high-endurance, long-range unmanned systems with Intelligence, Surveillance, and Reconnaissance (ISR), Electronic Warfare (EW), and lethal strike capabilities; and disruptive and less-lethal capabilities appropriate for countering malign activity by actors pursuing maritime "gray zone" strategies.[44]

Russian military thinkers have also followed discussions about the U.S. military's Joint Warfighting Concept and other efforts that outline U.S. views about future threats and force design. Russian analyses generally assume that the United States will attempt to conduct several actions that impact Russian force design:

■ Destroy early warning systems, air defense, missile defense, electronic warfare, and long-range precision weapons systems and capabilities;

■ Destroy or disable critical civilian and government installations, as well as key parts of the defense industrial base;

■ Disrupt command and control systems; and

■ Disrupt transport infrastructure facilities.[45]

The rest of this section examines five areas: land, air, maritime, space, and cyber.

Land: Russian force design in land warfare will likely focus on revitalizing the Russian army over the next five years.[46] Russia's offensive maneuver formations in Ukraine have been heavily weighted toward artillery, armor, support, and enablers rather than infantry. This structure has undermined Russia's ability to operate in urban terrain, support armor with dismounted infantry, conduct effective combined arms operations, and control terrain. There have also been shortages of key personnel, from enablers to logistics. The BTG structure is likely better suited to small-scale wars than to a large-scale conventional war.

Russian design of land forces may include several aspects, based on Russian military thinking.

First, there will likely be a continuing shift away from BTGs to divisions to prepare for deterrence and warfighting against NATO.[47] In particular, the Russian army will likely continue to move away from battalion formations to infantry, marine, and airborne divisions. This would mark a significant shift away from the changes implemented under former minister of defense Anatoly Serdyukov, who scrapped the Soviet-era structure of the armed forces that included large divisions as part of the "New Look" reforms.[48] A substantial number of Seryukov's changes are likely to be reversed over the next several years.

For example, Russian military leaders have indicated an intention to create at least nine new divisions: five artillery divisions, including super-heavy artillery brigades for building artillery reserves; two air assault divisions in the Russian Airborne Forces (VDV), bringing its force structure to roughly equal with Soviet times; and two motorized infantry divisions integrated into combined arms forces. The Ministry of Defense will likely transform seven motorized infantry brigades into motorized infantry divisions in the Western, Central, and Eastern Districts, as well as in the Northern Fleet. It will also likely expand an army corps in Karelia, across the border from Finland. In addition, each combined arms (tank) army may have a composite aviation division within it and an army aviation brigade with 80 to 100 combat helicopters under the control of ground force units—not the Russian Aerospace Forces. This decision was likely a result of the poor joint operations in Ukraine, especially air-land battle, though it does not fix poor coordination between Russian land and air forces.[49]

As part of a restructuring plan, the military also re-established the Moscow and Leningrad Military Districts as joint force strategic territorial units within the armed forces.[50] This was another blow to the Serdyukov "New Look" reforms, since he had condensed six military districts into four, as well as changed their command-and-control relationships.[51] The Western Military District's failure during the invasion of Ukraine may have contributed to its downfall. The Russian military will also likely increase the number of contract service members, or kontraktniki (контрактники), and raise the age ceiling for conscription.[52]

Second, the Russian army may experiment with different formations at the tactical level, according to some Russian military thinkers. During the war in Ukraine, Russian infantry structures at the tactical level have evolved from deploying uniform BTGs as combined arms units to a stratified division by function into line, assault, specialized, and disposable troops.[53] These infantry unit types might be formed into task-organized groupings in the future.

For example, *line units* could be largely used for holding territory and conducting defensive operations, and they could be based on mechanized units. They may not receive specific assault training, ensuring that they are largely used for defensive tasks. *Assault units* might include battalion-sized forces that are essentially reinforced battalions with a focus on urban and rural assault operations, including VDV and naval infantry units. They would receive additional training, perhaps akin to U.S. or other light infantry forces, and would likely be a skilled and valuable asset.[54] *Specialized* units, particularly infantry, could be generated through the normal Russian recruitment and training system, and they might include VDV or Spetsnaz. In ground combat, they would likely be held back from the front lines, fight from well-defended positions, and include snipers, artillery spotters, and support weapon operators. *Disposable units* might be drawn from local militias, private military companies, or under-trained mobilized Russian civilians. These forces might be assigned the initial advances to adversary positions and would likely be susceptible to high casualties. They could be used for skirmishing in order to identify adversary firing positions, which are then targeted by specialized infantry, or to find weak points in defenses that could be prioritized for assault.[55]

Third, the Russian army will likely attempt to restructure its units to allow for more mobility in the field.[56] The Russian Ministry of Defense has already indicated a desire to focus on motorized rifle and air assault divisions.[57] The evolution of Ukraine to a war of attrition has been costly for Russian ground forces. With the growth in non-contact warfare and long-range precision strike, concentrated forces are likely to be highly vulnerable in the future.[58] Some solutions for Russian units may include greater autonomy among soldiers at the squad, platoon, and company levels; standardized equipment among forces to maximize interchangeability; and a clearer understanding of the commander's intent before operations begin.[59] Each of these groups should have its own artillery mortars, field guns, launchers, UASs, and additional equipment.[60]

Fourth, Russian military thinkers have encouraged greater decentralization of Russian units, though this may be difficult in a military without a significant culture of delegation. Some assessments have concluded that Russian forces have lacked sufficient initiative in Ukraine because of poor training and command-and-control arrangements.[61] As one assessment noted, Russian "commanders of primary tactical units (platoon, squad, crew, or team) have poor skills in organizing and performing independent actions. This, in turn, leads to the fact that when command and control is excessively centralized during combat, military units instinctively gather in dense combat formations, marching columns, and concentration areas."[62] These problems can lead to "sluggishness, situational blindness, and vulnerability of the tactical or operational groups. As a result, an adversary with low density and network-structured combat formations . . . has an undeniable advantage over such unwieldy, sluggish, and vulnerable groups."[63]

Due to the over-centralization of Russia's military command structure in the early stages of the war in Ukraine, Russian officers deployed increasingly close to the front—even for brief visits. This risky decision made them targets for Ukrainian strikes and resulted in high casualties among senior officers. The loss of senior- and mid-level officers, who played a large role in tactical operations, undermined command-and-control and initiative at lower-unit levels. One proposed solution in Russian military thinking is a reduction in the size of active tactical units on the battlefield. A frontal assault might involve a reinforced motorized rifle battalion with extended intervals between squad, platoon, and company formations. According to one proponent of this structure, "One of the new features of modern combined arms combat (combat operations) is the reduction of the main, active tactical unit on the battlefield while increasing the number of such units.

The latter enjoy increased autonomy; in addition, they are homogeneous and independent, and horizontal coordination between them is important."[64]

Fifth, Russian land forces may struggle to restructure their relationship with non-state and quasi-state actors, including Russian private military companies. As already noted, Russian military analyses assume that Russia, like many of its competitors, will continue to work with irregular forces in future wars.[65] Following Prigozhin's insurrection in June 2023, however, the Russian military began an effort to reintegrate the Wagner Group and other contractors into the military. Following the death of Prigozhin in August 2023, almost certainly at Putin's instruction, the Russian government will likely attempt to reign in the Wagner Group and other private military companies under tighter Russian command-and-control.

Air: Force design in the air domain will also involve some reversals of reforms initiated by Serdyukov, as well as a major focus on UASs. Some of these changes are likely to be a reaction to problems encountered in Ukraine, while others are meant to deal with an expanded NATO viewed as a more significant threat and growing U.S. capabilities in global strike.[66]

In Ukraine, the Russian Aerospace Forces (Воздушно-космические силы, or VKS) has failed to achieve air superiority against a Ukrainian military with reasonable air defense capabilities, such as SA-10 and SA-11 surface-to-air missile systems, National Advanced Surface-to-Air Missile Systems (NASAMS), IRIS-T SL mobile air defense systems, and Patriot batteries. The success of Ukrainian air defenses, as well as the failure of Russian suppression of enemy air defense (SEAD) operations to take out Ukrainian air defense capabilities, has deterred Russian aircraft from operating over most of Ukrainian-controlled territory. This means that Russia's primary option to strike deep into Ukraine has been through cruise and ballistic missiles launched from Russia, Belarus, Russian-controlled territory in Ukraine, or maritime vessels in the Black Sea. In a war with U.S. and NATO forces, Russian air units would face an exponentially greater air defense threat.

As part of future restructuring, the Russian military has raised the possibility of increasing the size of the VKS by nine aviation regiments, including eight bomber regiments and one fighter regiment.[67] This addition would come on top of three existing bomber regiments and six fighter regiments, as well as five mixed regiments with fighter and ground-attack units, four long-range bomber squadrons, and one expeditionary fighter squadron. In addition, the Russian Ministry of Defense created three new operational commands of aviation divisions within the Russian air force.[68] This restructuring was a significant departure from the 2009 changes initiated by Serdyukov. He attempted to scrap the Russian air force's regimental structure inherited from the Soviet Union and to transition to the airbase as the main structural unit composed of squadrons. But Defense Minister Sergei Shoigu reversed several of Serdyukov's decisions, and an aviation regiment became roughly comparable to an airbase in size.[69]

In addition, the Russian military will likely expand the use of UASs into the overall plan for structuring, staffing, training, and equipping air forces—as well as land and maritime forces. The Russians are not alone. The evolution of UASs is one of the most significant components of future force design, including with the U.S. focus on a range of unmanned systems such as the collaborative combat aircraft, loitering munitions, and fully autonomous UASs. UASs are likely to be a critical part of Russia's reconnaissance-strike complex.

There are several Russian themes about unmanned systems and the future of warfare.

First, UASs may increasingly replace some types of missiles, artillery, and even fixed-wing aircraft for medium- and long-range strike for air, land, and maritime forces.[70] UASs will likely be integrated into key areas of the force, including land forces described in the previous section. According to some Russian assessments, future UASs with advances in precision, speed, payload, and range will likely offer several advantages over manned fixed-wing aircraft and helicopters: low radar visibility, an ability to perform most of the combat flight in complete silence, relatively low cost, and no casualties.[71] In addition, Russian military thinkers have also raised the possibility that UASs could operate in low Earth orbit, though it is unclear whether Russia has the technical capability to achieve this over the next three to five years. As one Russian analysis notes: "[U]nmanned aerospace attack weapons capable of operating both in air space and in outer space, performing numerous high-altitude maneuvers, will become widespread."[72]

Second, Russia is interested in utilizing unmanned systems for military logistics in contested environments, though the Russian military has not yet operationalized this capability.[73] An important goal is to develop and use UASs and other unmanned systems to deliver weapons, munitions, food, fuel, and other supplies to land, naval, and air forces. Used in this way, Russian forces would need to develop the necessary infrastructure, organizational structures, and processing systems to facilitate the use of UASs for logistics. As illustrated in Figure 3.3, there has been some Russian analysis about the different types and payloads necessary for cargo UASs.

The use of UASs for logistics will require new organizational structures. There is some consideration of a new special-purpose logistics service for the Russian military, as highlighted in Figure 3.4.

Figure 3.3: Main Types and Payloads of Proposed Russian Cargo UASs.

CARGO UASs	QUANTITY (UNITS)	PAYLOAD (METRIC TONS) up to 1	PAYLOAD (METRIC TONS) 1.1 to 4	PAYLOAD (METRIC TONS) 4 to 6	TOTAL PAYLOAD (METRIC TONS)
SQUADRON FREIGHT UAS					
Light	8	8	-	-	8
Medium	6	-	24	-	24
Heavy	4	-	-	24	24
Total	18	8	24	24	56

А. В. Топоров, М. С. Бондарь, Р. В. Ахметьянов [A.V. Toporov, M.S. Bondar, and R.V. Akhmetyanov], "Материально-техническая Поддержка В Бою И Операции: Проблемный Вопрос И Направления Его Разрешения" [Logistical Support in Combat and Operations: A Problem and Potential Solutions]," Военная мысль [Military Thought] 32, no. 2 (June 2023), 25.

Some Russian assessments judge that fixed-wing manned aircraft—especially fighter aircraft—may be less relevant in the future.[74] As one Russian assessment concluded:

▷ Unmanned aviation has gained prevalence in airspace over manned aviation in performing air reconnaissance and target acquisition. Special significance in performing strike missions both over the front line and in the depth of Ukrainian territory has been demonstrated by strike UAS capable of delivering considerable destruction to both small moving targets and large installations of Ukraine's critical infrastructure.[75]

There is considerable Russian interest in such U.S. programs as the Next Generation Air Dominance (NGAD) sixth-generation air superiority initiative, including a U.S. Air Force manned fighter aircraft and a supported unmanned collaborative combat aircraft using manned-unmanned teaming (MUM-T). To compete with the U.S. B-21, Russia will still likely continue its future long-range aviation complex (Prospective Aviation Complex of Long-Range Aviation, or PAK DA) project, with a subsonic low-observable flying wing and stealth capabilities.[76] Russia will also continue its next-generation Tu-160M Blackjack strategic bomber.[77] Some Russian analyses on sixth-generation aircraft emphasize the importance of developing technology that increases stealth; maximizes networking capabilities; integrates highly sensitive sensors; and develops hypersonic modes of flight, including near-space entry capability. For Russia, a major component of sixth-generation fighters is the "system of systems" concept to integrate aircraft into a broader system of surface ships, ground forces, command centers, satellites, and other manned and unmanned aircraft.[78]

Maritime: Unlike the army, the Russian navy remains largely intact. It lost the Black Sea flagship, the *Moskva*, and several auxiliaries. But Russia's four fleets—the Northern, Baltic, Black Sea, and Pacific Fleets—and Caspian Flotilla are still in reasonable shape. Nevertheless, Russia's future force design may evolve in several ways, based on a review of Russian military thinking.

First, Russian leaders have expressed an interest in strengthening Russian naval forces—including submarines—in response to growing tensions with the United States and NATO. The Ministry of Defense has announced a desire to create five naval infantry brigades for the navy's coastal troops based on existing naval infantry brigades.[79] This expansion followed Russia's adoption of a new maritime doctrine in July 2022, which identified the United States and NATO as major threats. In addition, the doctrine expressed an interest in building modern aircraft carriers, though it also highlighted the challenges of Russia's lack of overseas naval bases and the constraints on Russia's shipbuilding industry because of the West's economic sanctions.[80] Senior Russian officials have identified nuclear-powered submarines as critical in future force design.[81]

Second, the Russian navy will likely increase the presence of unmanned *maritime* vessels as part of force design. As one assessment notes: "Direct armed confrontation between ships will become predominantly auxiliary in nature. In the Navy, similar to the Aerospace Forces, the proportion of surface and submarine unmanned ships, both attack and support (reconnaissance, EW [electronic warfare], communications, transport), will increase significantly."[82] Along these lines, navies will likely position their crewed vessels—such as frigates, cruisers, corvettes, patrol boats, and destroyers—outside of the range of enemy fire and serve as control centers and carriers for unmanned vessels and UASs. Future warfare in the naval domain will increasingly involve armed confrontation between unmanned ships and UASs, including in swarms.

Space and Cyber: Military space and counterspace capabilities fall under the Russian Space Forces, which sits within the VKS.

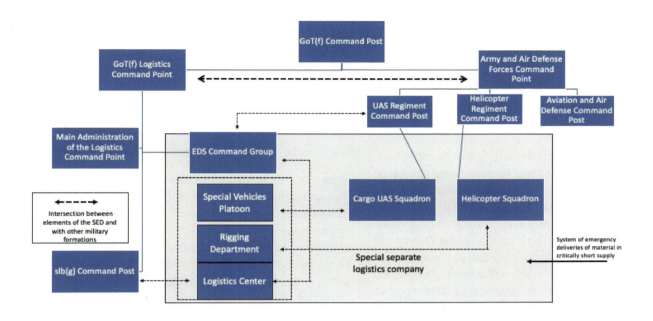

Figure 3.4: Diagram of the System for Cargo UASs.

А. В. Топоров, М. С. Бондарь, Р. В. Ахметьянов [A.V. Toporov, M.S. Bondar, and R.V. Akhmetyanov], "Материально-техническая поддержка в бою и операции: проблемный вопрос и направления" [Logistical Support in Combat and Operations: A Problem and Potential Solutions], Военная мысль [Military Thought] 32, no. 2 (June 2023): 17–31.

Russia will likely attempt to expand its counterspace capabilities, including kinetic physical weapons, such as direct-ascent anti-satellite weapons in low Earth orbit and co-orbital weapons; non-kinetic physical weapons, such as ground-based laser systems; electronic capabilities, including GPS jamming; and cyber intrusions.[83] However, there is little evidence that Russia is likely to implement any major changes in force design in the space domain, and Russia has been hampered by sanctions and a loss of international partnerships and funding.[84] One example of Russian struggles in the space domain was the August 2023 crash of the Luna-25 spacecraft, which was Russia's first space launch to the moon's surface since the 1970s.

Russia will likely attempt to expand its cyber capabilities under the GRU, SVR, and FSB, though Russia does not have a cyber command. The Presidential Administration and the Security Council coordinate cyber operations, but they are not a true cyber command. It is unclear whether Russia will create a veritable cyber command. What may be more likely is that Russian organizations, such as the GRU (including GRU Unit 26165, or the 85th Main Special Service Center), will recruit additional personnel, build new infrastructure, and increase their offensive cyber activities.

While a priority, Russian offensive cyber operations have failed to significantly blind Ukrainian command-and-control efforts or threaten critical infrastructure for a prolonged period. In the early phases of the invasion of Ukraine, for example, cyberattackers associated with the GRU, SVR, and FSB launched cyberattacks against hundreds of systems in the Ukrainian government and in Ukraine's energy, information technology, media, and financial sectors. Examples of Russian malware have included WhisperGate/WhisperKill, FoxBlade (or Hermetic Wiper), SonicVote (or HermeticRansom), and CaddyWiper.[85] But Russian cyber operations have failed to undermine Ukraine's ability or will to fight, in part because of outside state and non-state assistance to Ukraine to identify cyber and electronic warfare attacks, attribute attacks to the perpetrators, and assist with remediation.

In addition, a number of Russian military thinkers continue to focus on electronic warfare as a key aspect of force design.[86] This includes using the electromagnetic spectrum—such as radio, infrared, and radar—to sense, protect, and communicate, as well as to disrupt or deny adversaries the ability to use these signals. The demand for electronic warfare products will also likely trigger a growing push for electronic warfare technologies, including AI, so that electronic warfare systems can operate in the dense radio-frequency environment of the battlefield.

CONCLUSION

As this chapter argued, most Russian military thinkers believe that while the nature of warfare remains the same, the character of warfare is evolving in such areas as long-range, high-precision weapons; autonomous and unmanned systems; emerging technologies, such as AI; and the utility of non-state and quasi-state actors in warfare. In these and other areas, Russian leaders assess that it will be critical to cooperate with other countries, especially China. In addition, Russian political and military leaders are committed to a major reconstitution of the Russian military—especially the Russian army—over the next several years. Russia is likely to adopt a force design that centers around the division, yet also attempt to create forces that are more mobile and decentralized.

Achieving many of these goals will be challenging, if not impossible, as the next chapter explains. Russian leaders may want to make numerous changes, but they will be highly constrained. Russia faces a suite of financial, military, political, social, and other issues that will force political and military leaders to *prioritize* changes in force design. Building a bigger navy and air force will be expensive, as will increasing the size of Russian ground forces by 22 total divisions.[87] Moscow plans to boost its defense budget in 2024 to roughly 6 percent of gross domestic product, up from 3.9 percent in 2023.[88] But this increase will not be sufficient to implement all the changes Moscow's leaders have discussed.

While it is impossible to predict with certainty how Russian leaders will prioritize force design changes, likely candidates are ones that are relatively cheap or essential to improve fighting effectiveness.

Russia will likely prioritize rebuilding its army, which suffered significant attrition during the war in Ukraine and failed in numerous areas such as combined arms operations. Russia's army is essential to fight a protracted war in Ukraine and deter NATO. Indeed, it is difficult to envision Russia developing a modern force mix until it overhauls the army. Based on a review of Russian military assessments, it is reasonable to assume that the army will focus on restructuring its land forces around divisions; developing fires-centric capabilities, such as long-range artillery and laser-guided shells that maximize accuracy; and experimenting with tactical organizational structures that allow for greater mobility and autonomy against adversaries that have precision strike capabilities.

In the air domain, Russia will likely invest its limited resources in developing a broad suite of unmanned systems and long-range precision strike capabilities. UASs will likely be essential for future Russian warfighting to conduct a wide of missions, such as logistics in a contested environment, battlefield awareness, targeting for medium- and long-range fires, strike, information operations, and electronic warfare. In Ukraine, Russia increased the complexity, diversity, and density of UASs, with more lethal warheads and advances in noise reduction and counter-UAS capabilities. Russia will also continue to invest heavily in electronic warfare, based in part on successes of the Zhitel R330-Zh, Pole-21, and other systems in Ukraine.

In the maritime domain, Russia will likely focus on submarines and unmanned systems. Submarines are essential for Russia's nuclear deterrence posture. Of particular focus may be construction of the Project 955A (Borei-A) class of nuclear-powered ballistic missile submarines, which are built at the Sevmash shipyard in Severodvinsk. They are armed with Bulava submarine launched ballistic missiles, and Russia is continuing to develop technologies that reduce their acoustic signature. The Borei-class submarines will replace Russia's ageing, Soviet-era Delta III-class and Delta IV-class ballistic missile submarines.[89] More broadly, Russia is likely to prioritize maintenance of the nuclear triad, including its submarines, which is Moscow's main guarantee of security with a degraded conventional land force.

The Russian military will also likely focus on revitalizing its industrial base, with support from China, North Korea, Iran, and other countries. This means outsourcing some weapons systems (such as UASs) and components that Russian can't manufacture in sufficient quantities or lacks the technology or parts. As the war in Ukraine highlighted, an important prerequisite for offense and defense is fires dominance.[90] Russia will likely focus on building stockpiles of precision munitions for both Ukraine and NATO's eastern front.

The next chapter examines Russian challenges in implementing many of these reforms.

CONCLUSION

This chapter focuses on implications for the United States and NATO and makes two main arguments. First, Russian views of the future of warfare and efforts to restructure the military will likely be shaped by a strong view that the United States and NATO represent a clear and present threat to Moscow. The West's aid to Ukraine, expansion of NATO to Finland and likely Sweden, deployment of forces along NATO's eastern flank, and continuing military buildup will likely increase Moscow's perception of insecurity. Second, Moscow will likely face considerable challenges in implementing many of its changes. Moscow's lagging economy, rampant corruption, strained defense industrial base, and stovepiped military structure will likely create significant hurdles in implementing Russian force design goals. Despite these challenges, Russia still possesses some formidable capabilities with its strategic forces, navy, and air force.

The rest of this chapter is divided into three sections. The first examines the United States as Russia's main enemy. The second section assesses challenges in implementing Russian force design. The third provides a brief summary.

RUSSIA'S MAIN ENEMY

The United States—and NATO more broadly—will likely remain Russia's main enemy for the foreseeable future for at least two reasons.[1]

First, Russian political and military leaders assess that the country's struggles in Ukraine have been largely due to U.S. and broader NATO assistance.[2] As highlighted in Figure 4.1, the number of Russian soldiers killed in Ukraine during the first year of the war was greater than the *combined* number of Russian soldiers killed in all Russian and Soviet wars since World War II. As one senior Russian diplomat remarked about Ukraine, "The United States became a direct participant of this conflict long ago, and they have long been waging a hybrid war against my country. Ukraine is only an instrument in their hands, a tip of the spear held by the US-led collective West. Their goal is to destroy a sovereign, independent Russia as a factor in international politics."[3] This view that the United States and NATO are direct participants in the Ukraine war will likely persist and shape Moscow's views of the future of war and force design.

Second, Russian leaders believe that the United States is expanding its influence, attempting to further encircle Russia, and trying to weaken Russia militarily, politically, and economically.[4] NATO's June 2022 summit in Madrid also unambiguously stated that the "Russian Federation is the most significant and direct threat to Allies' security and to peace and stability in the Euro-Atlantic area."[5] In addition, the U.S. Department of Defense deployed or extended over 20,000 additional forces to Europe, bringing the total number of

Figure 4.1: Number of Soviet and Russian Soldiers Killed, 1950 to 2023[6]

Author's compilation. See endnotes for more details.

WAR	DATES	SOVIET AND RUSSIAN FORCES KILLED OR MISSING
Korea	1950-1953	120
Hungary	1956	669
United Arab Republic (Egypt)	1962-1963, 1969-1972, 1973-1974	21
Yemen Republic	1962-1963	1
Algeria	1962-1964	25
Vietnam	1965-1974	16
Mozambique	1967, 1969, 1975-1979	6
Czechoslovakia	1968	96
Sino-Soviet Border Conflict	1969	58
Angola	1975-1979	7
Ethiopia	1977-1990	34
Afghanistan	1979-1989	14,000-16,000
Chechnya (First and Second Wars)	1994-1996, 1999-2009	12,000-25,000
Georgia	2008	64
Ukraine (Crimea and Donbas)	2014-February 2022	6,000-7,000
Syria	2015-Present	264
Ukraine	February 2022-Present	120,000-140,000

U.S. personnel in Europe to over 100,000. Examples included the deployment of an Armored Brigade Combat Team, a High-Mobility Rocket Artillery Battalion (HIMARS) battalion, and KC-135 refueling aircraft, among other forces. Other steps of concern to Russia have included:

- A permanent forward station of V Corps Headquarters Forward Command Post, an Army garrison headquarters, and a field support battalion in Poland;
- The deployment of an additional rotational brigade combat team in Romania;
- Enhanced rotational deployments in the Baltics;
- An increase in the number of destroyers stationed at Rota, Spain, from four to six;
- The forward stationing of two F-35 squadrons in the United Kingdom;
- The forward stationing of an air defense artillery brigade headquarters, a short-range air defense battalion, a combat sustainment support battalion headquarters, and an engineer brigade headquarters in Germany; and
- The forward stationing of a short-range air defense battery in Italy.

While these steps are a *reaction* to Russia's invasion of Ukraine and entirely legitimate, they have increased Russian fears of encirclement. As Defense Minister Sergei Shoigu remarked at the December 2022 meeting of Russian's Defense Ministry Board, "Of particular concern is the buildup of NATO's advance presence near the borders of the Russian Federation and the Republic of Belarus . . . to further weaken our country." Shoigu also noted, "Considering NATO's aspirations to build up its military capabilities close to the Russian border, as well as expand the alliance by accepting Finland and Sweden as new members, we need to respond by creating a corresponding group of forces in Russia's northwest."[7]

The result is that the Russia's insecurity and animosity toward the West—and the United States in particular—will likely deepen. These sentiments will likely drive a desire to reconstitute the Russian military over the next several years, strengthen nuclear and conventional deterrence, and prepare to fight the West if deterrence fails. Russian military thinking on the future of warfare and force design is dominated by a view that the United States is—and will remain—Moscow's primary enemy.

CHALLENGES TO FORCE DESIGN

Russia faces enormous challenges in implementing its force design, despite its ambitions. Russia's military almost certainly lacks the caliber of some of the great historical Russian and Soviet military thinkers, such as Mikhail Tuchachevsky, Aleksandr Svechin, Vladimir Triandafilov, and Georgii Isserson. As noted earlier in this report, Russian military journals generally lack innovative thought and self-criticism, almost certainly a result of Russia's increasingly authoritarian climate. In addition, Russia's military has been unable to attract the best and brightest of young Russians in the face of competition from the civilian labor market, despite some pay raises.[8]

There are at least five additional challenges to Russian force design over the next several years.

First, Russia's deepening economic crisis will likely constrain its efforts to expand the quantity and quality of its ground, air, and naval forces. The war in Ukraine has fueled Russia's worst labor crunch in decades; hundreds of thousands of workers have fled the country or have been sent to fight in Ukraine, weakening an economy weighed down by economic sanctions and international isolation. The country's biggest exports—gas and oil—have lost major customers. Government finances have been strained and the ruble has decreased against the dollar.[9] Numerous Western banks, investors, and companies have fled Russia and its financial markets. In addition, the International Monetary Fund has estimated that Russia's potential growth rate—the rate at which it could grow without courting inflation—was around 3.5 percent before 2014, the year Russia seized Crimea, but fell to around roughly 0.7 percent in 2023 as productivity declined and the economy became increasingly isolated.[10] The fall in exports, tight labor market, and increased government spending have worsened inflation risks.

Russian force design will not be cheap. The Russian army wants to create new divisions and recruit additional soldiers, which will drive up costs because of salaries, signing bonuses, healthcare, lodging, food, equipment, and other factors. Russia will need to make military service more attractive. For example, housing remains a problem for Russian officers with families, and salaries have not kept pace with inflation for several years.[11] The development and production of emerging technologies can be enormously expensive. So are major platforms, such as bombers, submarines, aircraft carriers, and fifth- and sixth-generation aircraft.

Second, corruption remains rampant in the Russian military, which could undermine Moscow's overall plan to structure, staff, train, and equip its forces. Corruption has long been a problem in the Russian military.[12] In Ukraine, the Russian military has provided some soldiers on the front lines with ration packs that were seven years old, other soldiers have crowdsourced for body armor because Russian supplies dried up, some have sold fuel on the black market that was intended for Russian main battle tanks and other vehicles, and supply chains have failed.[13] Russian morale likely has suffered. Russian soldiers have also engaged in false reporting, committed outright theft, overstated the number of enlistees in some units (and skimmed the difference), and conducted other forms of graft.[14] Corruption in the Russian military is not surprising. According to some estimates, one-fifth or more of the Russian Ministry of Defense's budget is siphoned off by officials.[15] These factors help explain why former Russian foreign minister Andrei Kozyrev referred to the Russian armed forces as a "Potemkin military."[16]

Third, Russia's defense industrial base will likely face at least two types of challenges which could impact force design. One is replacement of losses from the war in Ukraine. Russia has already expended significant amounts of precision-guided and other munitions in the Ukraine war, and many of its weapons and equipment have been destroyed or severely worn down. According to some estimates, for example, Russia lost approximately 50 percent of its modern T-72B3 and T-72B3M main battle tanks over the first year of the war, along with roughly two-thirds of its T-80BV/U tanks.[17] A protracted war in Ukraine will likely compound these challenges. Replacing these losses will be necessary before implementing new initiatives or building new forces.

Another challenge is that economic sanctions will likely create shortages of higher-end foreign components and may force Moscow to substitute them with lower-quality alternatives. These challenges could impact Russia's ability to manufacture, sustain, and produce advanced weapons and technology.[18] As Russia's 2022 maritime doctrine concluded, one of the main risks to Russia's maritime activities is "the introduction of restrictions, which include the transfer of modern technologies, deliveries of equipment and attraction of long-term investments, imposed by a number of states against Russian shipbuilding enterprises of the defense industrial complex and oil and gas companies."[19] Supply-chain problems have also delayed deliveries. Money to replace outdated machine tools and pay for research and development is lacking, while neglect of quality control is common.[20] Continuing assistance from China, Iran, North Korea, and other countries could help ameliorate some of these challenges.

Fourth, Russia may face a significant challenge because of growing civil-military tension. As Harvard political scientist Samuel Huntington wrote in his book *The Soldier and the State*, "The military institutions of any society are shaped by two forces: a functional imperative stemming from the threats to the society's security and a societal imperative arising from the social forces, ideologies, and institutions dominant within the society."[21] The need to balance military institutions and societal forces is no less true for Russia today. It is conceivable that tension between the Russian military and population could worsen over time because of a protracted war in Ukraine, a languishing economy, and an increasingly authoritarian state.

The June 2023 rebellion led by Yevgeny Prigozhin was one indicator of domestic frustration, although it is difficult to assess the breadth and depth of popular anger. A reconstitution of the Russian military will likely require some level of support and sacrifice from the Russian population.

Fifth, Russia has struggled to coordinate strategy and operations across its services. Russian military exercises are often stovepiped, with poor coordination and limited jointness across the army, air force, and navy. The Russian military has failed to effectively conduct joint operations in Ukraine. These challenges raise major questions about whether the Russian military can create a truly joint force.

CONCLUSION

In the months before Russia's invasion of Ukraine, U.S. government assessments were generally accurate in predicting that Russian forces would invade Ukraine. But many were wrong in their assessment of the war's outcome. Most assumed that Russian forces would defeat Ukrainian forces in a matter of days or weeks. But they overstated the effectiveness of Russian forces and understated the will to fight, combined arms capabilities, leadership, and morale of Ukrainian forces, political leaders, and the population. These errors may have occurred because it is generally easier to analyze tangible aspects of a military, such as doctrine and air, land, naval, cyber, and space capabilities, but much more difficult to assess the intangible aspects of warfare, including morale, will to fight, readiness, impact of corruption, and force employment.

These analytical challenges raise important questions about how to assess Russian military reconstitution, views on the future of warfare, and force design. Moving forward, U.S. and allied policymakers should routinely ask and attempt to answer several questions regarding Russian views of warfare and force design:

- How will Russia attempt to improve the "intangibles" of warfare, such as the will to fight and readiness?
- How will Russia prioritize its force design ambitions given its many competing needs?
- Can Russia continue to secure significant support from China, Iran, North Korea, and other countries for its military, including technology, weapons systems, and money? How might such support impact force design?
- Can Russia overcome historic problems, such as corruption? If so, how?

While there may be a temptation to examine Russian views of the future of warfare primarily through a Ukraine lens, this would be a mistake. The war in Ukraine has impacted Russian military thinking, but it is only one war at one point in time.

In his book *Strategy*, Russian military leader and theorist Alexander Svechin remarked that "each war has to be matched with a special strategic behavior; each war constitutes a particular case that requires establishing its own special logic instead of applying some template."[22] Svechin believed in the uniqueness of war. The challenge in understanding Russian thinking about the future of warfare is to step back and attempt to understand how Russian leaders view the evolving international environment and to how they can best maximize their security given the resources at their disposal.

ABOUT THE AUTHOR

SETH G. JONES is senior vice president, Harold Brown Chair, director of the International Security Program, and director of the Transnational Threats Project at the Center for Strategic and International Studies (CSIS). He focuses on defense strategy, military operations, force posture, and irregular warfare. He leads a bipartisan team of over 50 resident staff and an extensive network of non-resident affiliates dedicated to providing independent strategic insights and policy solutions that shape national security. He also teaches at Johns Hopkins University's School of Advanced International Studies (SAIS) and the Center for Homeland Defense and Security (CHDS) at the U.S. Naval Postgraduate School.

Prior to joining CSIS, Dr. Jones was the director of the International Security and Defense Policy Center at the RAND Corporation. He also served as representative for the commander, U.S. Special Operations Command, to the assistant secretary of defense for special operations. Before that, he was a plans officer and adviser to the commanding general, U.S. Special Operations Forces, in Afghanistan (Combined Forces Special Operations Component Command-Afghanistan). In 2014, Dr. Jones served on a congressionally mandated panel that reviewed the FBI's implementation of counterterrorism recommendations contained in the 9/11 Commission Report. He is the author of *Three Dangerous Men: Russia, China, Iran, and the Rise of Irregular Warfare* (W.W. Norton, 2021), *A Covert Action: Reagan, the CIA, and the Cold War Struggle in Poland* (W.W. Norton, 2018), *Waging Insurgent Warfare: Lessons from the Vietcong to the Islamic State* (Oxford University Press, 2016), *Hunting in the Shadows: The Pursuit of al Qa'ida since 9/11* (W.W. Norton, 2012), and *In the Graveyard of Empires: America's War in Afghanistan* (W.W. Norton, 2009). Dr. Jones has published articles in a range of journals, such as *Foreign Affairs*, *Foreign Policy*, and *International Security*, as well as newspapers and magazines like the *New York Times*, *Washington Post*, and *Wall Street Journal*. Dr. Jones is a graduate of Bowdoin College and received his MA and PhD from the University of Chicago.

ENDNOTES

Introductory Quote

1. Александр Андреевич Свечин [Alexander Andreyevich Svechin], Стратегия [*Strategy*] (Moscow: Gosvoenizdat, 1926), 8.

Chapter 1: Introduction

1. Russia has also used other concepts. "Force development," for example, is the set of interconnected economic, sociopolitical, information, psychological, ideological, military, and other activities conducted by Russian military and political leadership to establish a military organization and ensure its continuous development and functioning for the purpose of defense and security. А. В. Смоловый, А. В. Павловский [A.V. Smolovy and A.V. Pavlovsky], "Методика Оценки Боевых Возможностей Группировок Войск (Сил) На Стратегических Направлениях" [Methodology for Assessing the Combat Potential of Troop (Force) Groupings in Strategic Sectors], Военная Мысль [*Military Thought*] 32, no. 2 (June 2023): 32-46.

Chapter 2: The Historical Context

1. For an overview of Soviet thinking, see Dima Adamsky, *The Culture of Military Innovation: The Impact of Cultural Factors on the Revolution in Military Affairs in Russia, the U.S., and Israel* (Stanford, CA: Stanford University Press, 2010), 24-57.

2. Николай Васильевич Огарков [Nikolai Vasilyevich Ogarkov], Всегда в готовности к защите Отечества [*Always in Readiness to Defend the Fatherland*] (Moscow: Voennoe Izdatel'stvo, 1982), 31-43, 59-67.

3. Adamsky, *The Culture of Military Innovation*, 33.

4. Николай Васильевич Огарков [Nikolai Vasilyevich Ogarkov], "Надежная защита мира" [A Reliable Defense to Peace], Красная звезда [*Red Star*], September 23, 1983, 2.

5. Николай Васильевич Огарков [Nikolai Vasilyevich Ogarkov], "Защита социализма: опыт истории и современность" [Defense of Socialism: The Experience of History and the Present], Красная звезда [*Red Star*], May 9, 1984, 2-3. Also see Николай Васильевич Огарков [Nikolai Vasilyevich Ogarkov], История учит бдительность [*History Teaches Vigilance*] (Moscow: Voyenizdat, 1985), 51.

6. Сергей Чекинов, Сергей Богданов [Sergey Chekinov and Sergey Bogdanov], "О характере и содержании войны нового поколения" [The Nature and Content of a New-Generation War], Военная мысль [*Military Thought*] 22, no. 4 (2013).

7. Валерии Герасимов [Valery Gerasimov], "Влияние современного характера вооруженной борьбы на направленность строительства и развития Вооруженных Сил Российской Федерации. Приоритетные задачи военной науки в обеспечении обороны страны" [The Influence of the Contemporary Nature of Armed Struggle on the Focus of the Construction and Development of the Armed Forces of the Russian Federation. Priority Tasks of Military Science in Safeguarding the Country's Defense], Вестник Академии Военных Наук [*Journal of the Academy of Military Sciences*] 62, no. 2 (2018).

8. Michael Kofman et al., *Russian Military Strategy: Core Tenets and Operational Concepts* (Arlington, VA: Center for Naval Analyses, August 2021), https://www.cna.org/archive/CNA_Files/pdf/russian-military-strategy-core-tenets-and-operational-concepts.pdf.

9. Владимир Слипченко [Vladimir Slipchenko], Войны нового поколения. Дистанционные и бесконтактные [*Wars of the New Generation: Remote and Contactless*] (Moscow: OLMA-Press, 2004); Владимир Слипченко [Vladimir Slipchenko], Бесконтактные войны

[*Contactless Wars*] (Moscow: Izdatel'skii dom: Gran-Press, 2001); and Владимир Слипченко [Vladimir Slipchenko], Война будущего [*War of the Future*] (Moscow: Moskovskii Obshchestvennyi Nauchnyi Fond, 1999).

10. Виктор Рябчук [Viktor Ryabchuk], "Изучение и методология военной науки" [Study and Methodology of Military Science], Русская Мысль [*Russian Thought*], no. 6 (November-December 2001).

11. Gerasimov, "The Influence of the Contemporary Nature of Armed Struggle"; Valery Gerasimov, "Remarks by Chief of General Staff of the Russian Federation General of the Army Valery Gerasimov at the Russian Defence Ministry's Board Session," Ministry of Defence of the Russian Federation, November 7, 2017; and Виктор Худолеев [Viktor Khudoleev], "Военная наука смотрит в будущее" [Military Science Looks to the Future], Красная звезда [*Red Star*], March 26, 2018, http://archive.redstar.ru/index.php/component/k2/item/36626-voennaya-nauka-smotrit-v-budushchee.

12. Dmitry (Dima) Adamsky, "Russian Lessons from the Syrian Operation and the Culture of Military Innovation," *Security Insights*, no. 47 (February 2020), https://www.marshallcenter.org/en/publications/security-insights/russian-lessons-syrian-operation-and-culture-military-innovation; and Roger McDermott, *Russia's Entry to Sixth-Generation Warfare: The 'Non-Contact' Experiment in Syria* (Washington, DC: Jamestown Foundation, May 29, 2021), https://jamestown.org/program/russias-entry-to-sixth-generation-warfare-the-non-contact-experiment-in-syria.

13. Timothy Thomas, *Russian Combat Capabilities for 2020: Three Developments to Track* (McLean, VA: MITRE, December 2019), 12, https://www.armyupress.army.mil/Portals/7/Legacy-Articles/documents/Thomas-Russian-Combat-Capabilities.pdf.

14. О. С. Таненя, В. Н. Урюпин [O.S. Tanenya and V.N. Uryupin], "К Вопросу Применения Воздушных Десантов [Using Airborne Forces]," Военная мысль [*Military Thought*] 26, no. 3 (2017).

15. Ralph Shield, "Russian Airpower's Success in Syria: Assessing Evolution in Kinetic Counterinsurgency," *Journal of Slavic Military Studies* 31, no. 2 (2018): 214-39, doi:10.1080/13518046.2018.1451099; Tom Cooper, "Here's the Key to Understanding the Russian Air Force's Actions in Syria," War Is Boring, June 6, 2016, https://medium.com/war-is-boring/heres-the-key-to-understanding-the-russian-air-force-s-actions-in-syria-68aa3e4f8d0d Robert Lee, "Russia's Military Operation in Syria," *Armed Forces*, Moscow Defense Brief No. 2, 2017, 11; and Michael Simpson et al., *Road to Damascus: The Russian Air Campaign in Syria, 2015 to 2018* (Santa Monica, CA: RAND, 2022), 26, https://www.rand.org/pubs/research_reports/RRA1170-1.html.

16. Shield, "Russian Airpower's Success in Syria," 214-39.

17. Ibid., 214-39.

18. Валерии Герасимов [Valery Gerasimov], "Развитие Военной Стратегии В Современных Условиях. Задачи Военной Науки" [Development of Military Strategy in Modern Conditions. Tasks of Military Science], Вестник Академии Военных Наук [*Journal of the Academy of Military Sciences*] 67, no. 2 (2019).

19. Александр Андреевич Свечин [Alexander Andreyevich Svechin], Стратегия [*Strategy*] (Moscow: Gosvoenizdat, 1926), 8.

20. Kofman et al., *Russian Military Strategy*.

21. Михаил Барабанова [Mikhail Barabanov], ed., Новая армия России [*Russia's New Army*]

(Moscow: Center for Analysis of Strategies and Technologies, 2011).

22   Михаил Барабанова [Mikhail Barabonov], "Реформа боевого духа" [Morale Reform], Коммерсантъ Власть [*Kommersant-Vlast*], October 20, 2008.

23   Mark Galeotti, *The Modern Russian Army 1992-2016* (New York: Osprey, 2017), 27.

24   Michael Kofman and Rob Lee, "Not Built for Purpose: The Russian Military's Ill-Fated Force Design," War on the Rocks, June 2, 2022, https://warontherocks.com/2022/06/not-built-for-purpose-the-russian-militarys-ill-fated-force-design/.

25   Mark Galeotti, *The Modern Russian Army 1992-2016* (New York: Osprey, 2017), 28.

26   Ibid., 28.

27   Lester Grau and Charles K. Bartles, "Getting to Know the Russian Battalion Tactical Group," Royal United Services Institute, April 14, 2022, https://rusi.org/explore-our-research/publications/commentary/getting-know-russian-battalion-tactical-group; Mark Galeotti, *Armies of Russia's War in Ukraine* (New York: Osprey, 2019); and Ibid.

28   Grau and Bartles, "Getting to Know the Russian Battalion Tactical Group."

29   Seth G. Jones, *Three Dangerous Men: Russia, China, Iran, and the Rise of Irregular Warfare* (New York: W.W. Norton, 2021).

30   Frank Hoffman, "'Hybrid Threats:' Neither Omnipotent Nor Unbeatable," *Orbis* 54, no. 3 (2010): 441-55; and Ofer Fridman, *Russian Hybrid Warfare: Resurgence and Politicisation* (New York: Oxford University Press, 2018).

31   Stephen Biddle, *Nonstate Warfare: The Military Methods of Guerillas, Warlords, and Militias* (Princeton, NJ: Princeton University Press, 2021).

32   The al-Quds force appeared to receive training from a Russian PMC called Vegacy Strategic Services. See, for example, Ruslan Leviev, "A New PMC From Ukraine Has Appeared in Syria," Citeteam, March 2019, https://citeam.org/pmc-vega/?lang=R; and Kofman and Rojansky, "What Kind of Victory for Russia in Syria?"

33   Ibid.

34   Ruslan Leviev, "They Fought for Palmyra… Again: Russian Mercenaries Killed in Battle With ISIS," CiteTeam, March 2017, https://citeam.org/they-fought-for-palmyra-again-russian-mercenaries-killed-in-battle-with-isis/?lang=en.

35   See, for example, Seth G. Jones et al., *Russia's Corporate Soldiers: The Global Expansion of Russia's Private Military Companies* (Lanham, MD: Rowman & Littlefield, 2021), https://www.csis.org/analysis/russias-corporate-soldiers-global-expansion-russias-private-military-companies.

Chapter 3: The Future of Warfare and Russian Force Design

1   See, for example, Сергей Чекинов, Сергей Богданов [Sergey Chekinov and Sergey Bogdanov], "Эволюция сущности и содержания понятия 'война' в XXI столетии" [The Essence and Content of the Evolving Notion of War in the 21st Century], Военная мысль [*Military Thought*] 26, no. 1 (2017): 74.

2   Carl von Clausewitz, *On War* (New York: Penguin Books, 1968), 101.

3   В. Г. Цилько, А. А. Иванов [V.G. Tsilko and A.A. Lvanov], "Тенденции Развития Общевойскового Оперативного Искусства [Developments in Combined Arms Operational

Art]," Военная мысль [*Military Thought*] 32, no. 1 (March 2023): 39-47. Also see И. Л. Макарчук, К. А. Троценко [I.L. Makarchuk and K.A. Trotsenko], "Характер Операций Современных Армий - Назревшие Изменения" [The Nature of Operations of Modern Armies: Overdue Change], Военная мысль [*Military Thought*] 32, no. 1 (March 2023): 85-99.

4   А. В. Сержантов, А. В. Смоловый, И. А. Терентьев [A.V. Serzhantov, A.V. Smolovy, and I.A. Terentyev], "Трансформация Содержания Войны: Контуры Военных Конфликтов Будущего" [Transformation of the Content of War: Outlining Military Conflicts of the Future], Военная мысль [*Military Thought*] 31, no. 4 (December 2022): 57-68.

5   For a historical view on the reconnaissance-strike complex, see Валерии Герасимов [Valery Gerasimov], "Влияние современного характера вооруженной борьбы на направленность строительства и развития Вооруженных Сил Российской Федерации. Приоритетные задачи военной науки в обеспечении обороны страны" [The Influence of the Contemporary Nature of Armed Struggle on the Focus of the Construction and Development of the Armed Forces of the Russian Federation. Priority Tasks of Military Science in Safeguarding the Country's Defense], Вестник Академии Военных Наук [*Journal of the Academy of Military Sciences*] 62, no. 2 (2018).

6   О.В. Ермолин, Н.П. Зубов, М.В. Фомин [O.V. Yermolin, N.P. Zubov, and M.V. Fomin], "Применение Ударной Авиации Воздушно-космических Сил В Военных Конфликтах Будущего" [Use of Aerospace Forces' Strike Aviation in Future Military Conflicts], Военная мысль [*Military Thought*] 32, no. 2 (June 2023): 81-93.

7   Chekinov and Bogdanov, "The Essence and Content of the Evolving Notion of War in the 21st Century," 37.

8   Makarchuk and Trotsenko, "The Nature of Operations of Modern Armies: Overdue Change."

9   Tsilko and A.A. Lvanov, "Developments in Combined Arms Operational Art." Also see Makarchuk and Trotsenko, "The Nature of Operations of Modern Armies: Overdue Change."

10 See, for example, Мариам Мохаммад, В. Н. Похващев, Л. Б. Рязанцев [Mariam Mohammad, V.N. Pokhvashchev, and L.B. Ryazantsev], "К Вопросу Повышения Эффективности Противодействия Малоразмерным Беспилотным Летательным Аппаратам" [Improving the Efficiency of Countering Small Unmanned Aerial Vehicles], Военная мысль [*Military Thought*] 31, no. 4 (December 2022): 69-77; and Г.А. Лопин, Г.И. Смирнов, И.Н. Ткачёв [G.A. Lopin, G.I. Smirnov, and I.N. Tkachov], "Развитие Средств Борьбы С Беспилотными Летательными Аппаратами" [Development of Assets to Counter Unmanned Vehicles], Военная мысль [*Military Thought*] 32, no. 2 (June 2023): 58-67.

11 "Meeting of Defense Ministry Board," National Defense Control Center, Moscow, December 21, 2022, http://en.kremlin.ru/events/president/transcripts/70159.

12 On the United States and drones see, for example, А.В. Когтин, Г. Я. Шайдуров [A.V. Kogtin and G. Ya. Shaidurov], "Перспективы развития малых беспилотных летательных аппаратов и проблема их обнаружения" [Development Prospects for Small Unmanned Aerial Vehicles and the Problem of Detecting Them], Военная мысль [*Military Thought*] 32, no. 2 (June 2023): 142-46; and Lopin, Smirnov, and Tkachov, "Development of Assets to Counter Unmanned Vehicles."

13 Lopin, Smirnov, and Tkachov, "Development of Assets to Counter Unmanned Vehicles"; А. С. Уланов [A.S. Ulanov], "Прогностическая Оценка Тенденций Развития Средств Вооруженной Борьбы И Способов Их Применения В Войнах Будущего" [Forecast of Trends in the Development of Military Assets and Their Use in Future Wars], Военная мысль [*Military Thought*] 31, no. 4 (December 2022): 94-110; and В. Б. Зарудницкий

[Z.B. Zarudnitsky], "Факторы Достижения Победы В Военных Конфликтах Будущего" [Factors in Achieving Victory in Future Military Conflicts], Военная мысль [*Military Thought*] 30, no. 1 (2021): 39-54.

14 On AI and drones, see В.М. Иванец, В.Н. Лукьянчик, В.Н. Мельник [V.M. Ivanets, V.N. Lukyanchik, and V.N. Melnik], "Особенности управления дронами как частью интеллектуального беспилотного авиационного комплекса на основе технологий искусственного интеллекта" [Specific Features of Controlling Drones as Part of Intelligence Unmanned Aircraft System Based on Artificial Intelligence Technologies], Военная мысль [*Military Thought*] 32, no. 1 (March 2023): 143-52.

15 Mohammad, Pokhvashchev, and Ryazantsev, "Improving the Efficiency of Countering Small Unmanned Aerial Vehicles," 71.

16 Ulanov, "Forecast of Trends."

17 Lopin, Smirnov, and Tkachov, "Development of Assets to Counter Unmanned Vehicles."

18 Kogtin and Shaidurov, "Development Prospects for Small Unmanned Aerial Vehicles"; В. Н. Тикшаев, В. В. Барвиненко [V.N. Tikshayev and V.V. Barvinenko], "Проблема Борьбы С Беспилотными Летательными Аппаратами И Возможные Пути Ее Решения" [The Problem of Fighting Unmanned Aerial Vehicles and Possible Solutions], Военная мысль [*Military Thought*] 30, no. 2 (2021): 49-58.

19 Michael C. Horowitz, *The Diffusion of Military Power: Causes and Consequences for International Politics* (Princeton, NJ: Princeton University Press, 2010), 221-22.

20 Kogtin and Shaidurov, "Development Prospects for Small Unmanned Aerial Vehicles."

21 Ibid.

22 Ibid., 145.

23 Lopin, Smirnov, and Tkachov, "Development of Assets to Counter Unmanned Vehicles"; and С. И. Макаренко [S.I. Makarenko], Противодействие беспилотным летательным аппаратам: монография [*Countermeasures against Unmanned Aerial Vehicles: A Monograph*] (St. Petersburg, Russia: Science-Intensive Technologies Publishers, 2020).

24 Mohammad, Pokhvashchev, and Ryazantsev, "Improving the Efficiency of Countering Small Unmanned Aerial Vehicles," 71.

25 Д.В. Галкин, В.Н. Дятлов, А.В. Степанов [D.V. Galkin, V.N. Dyatlov, and A.V. Stepanov], "Перспективные Военно-прикладные Технологии" [Advanced Military Applied Technologies], Военная мысль [*Military Thought*] 31, no. 3 (September 2022): 117-23; Ulanov, "Forecast of Trends"; П. А. Дульнев, А. В. Котов, Н. П. Педенко [P.A. Dulnev, A.V. Kotov, and N.P. Pedenko], "Прогнозирование Хода И Исхода Общевойскового Боя Как Метод Теории Общей Тактики" [Forecasting the Course and Outcome of Combined Arms Combat as a Method of General Tactics Theory], Военная мысль [*Military Thought*] 32, no. 2 (June 2023): 94-105; and Tsilko and Lvanov, "Developments in Combined Arms Operational Art."

26 "Pantsir systems demonstrated effectiveness in Ukraine - Rostec," TASS, March 25, 2022, https://tass.com/defense/1427385; and Tsilko and Lvanov, "Developments in Combined Arms Operational Art."

27 Ulanov, "Forecast of Trends."

28 See, for example, "Future of global arms market lies with robots, AI – Russian defense exporter," TASS, May 22, 2023, https://tass.com/defense/1621221; "Putin highlights need to integrate combat drones into single network," TASS, December 21, 2022, https://tass.com/defense/1553969; and "ФПИ предложил Минобороны стандарты для искусственного интеллекта" [FPI Proposed to the Ministry of Defence Standards for Artificial Intelligence] РИА Новости [RIA Novosti], March 20, 2018, https://ria.ru/20180320/1516808875.html.

29 Galkin, Dyatlov, and Stepanov, "Advanced Military Applied Technologies"; Yermolin, Zubov, and Fomin, "Use of Aerospace Forces' Strike Aviation in Future Military Conflicts"; and А. В. Хомутов [A.V. Khomutov], "О Противодействии Противнику В Условиях Ведения Им 'Многосферных Операций'" [Countering the Multi-Domain Operations of the Adversary], Военная мысль [*Military Thought*] 30, no. 5 (2021).

30 Ulanov, "Forecast of Trends," 98.

31 Galkin, Dyatlov, and Stepanov, "Advanced Military Applied Technologies."

32 See, for example, Ulanov, "Forecast of Trends"; В. Е. Харченко, Р.П. Калуцкий [V. Ye. Kharchenko and R.P. Kalutsky], "Об Оценке Вклада Группировки Сил И Средств Радиоэлектронной Борьбы В Снижение Боевого Потенциала Противника" [Assessing the Contribution of an Electronic Warfare Grouping to the Reduction of Enemy Combat Capabilities], Военная мысль [*Military Thought*] 32, no. 1 (March 2023): 120-28; and Galkin, Dyatlov, and Stepanov, "Advanced Military Applied Technologies."

33 Евгений Куценко, Кирилл Тюрчев, Татьяна Остащенко [Evgeniy Kutsenko, Kirill Tyurchev, and Tatyana Ostashchenko], "Релокация как драйвер инновационной активности: глобальное исследование международной миграции основателей компаний-единорогов" [Relocation as a Driver of Innovative Activity: A Global Study of Unicorn Founders' Migration], Форсайт [*Foresight*] 16, no. 4 (2022): 6-23, https://foresight-journal.hse.ru/data/2022/12/14/1715770690/1-%D0%9A%D1%83%D1%86%D0%B5%D0%BD%D0%BA%D0%BE-6-23.pdf.

34 See, for example, Masha Borak, "How Russia Killed Its Tech Industry," *MIT Technology Review*, April 4, 2023, https://www.technologyreview.com/2023/04/04/1070352/ukraine-war-russia-tech-industry-yandex-skolkovo/.

35 А.А. Бартош [A.A. Bartosh], "Законы и принципы гибридной войны" [Laws and Principles of Hybrid Warfare], Военная мысль [*Military Thought*] 32, no. 1 (March 2023): 11-20; Serzhantov, Smolovy, and Terentyev, "Transformation of the Content of War"; and Tsilko and Lvanov, "Developments in Combined Arms Operational Art."

36 In Syria, Iran and the Islamic Revolutionary Guard Corps-Quds Force played a central role in Russian cooperation with Lebanese Hezbollah and militias composed of fighters from Palestinian territory, Syria, Iraq, Afghanistan, Pakistan, and other locations.

37 Tsilko and Lvanov, "Developments in Combined Arms Operational Art."

38 Bartosh, "Laws and Principles of Hybrid Warfare"; Валерии Герасимов [Valery Gerasimov], "Современные войны и актуальные вопросы организации обороны страны" [Contemporary Warfare and Current Issues for the Defense of the Country], Вестник Академии Военных Наук [*Journal of the Academy of Military Sciences*] 2, no. 59 (2017).

39 See, for example, "Russia becomes target of West's coordinated aggression in cyberspace - MFA," TASS, January 28, 2023, https://tass.com/russia/1568405.

40 Константин Сивков [Konstantin Sivkov], "Украина—только начало: Геополитическим

последствием спецоперации станет изменение" [Ukraine is just the beginning: The geopolitical consequences of the special operation will change the entire view of the world], Военно-промышленный курьер [*Military-Industrial Courier*], March 28, 2022; and Zarudnitsky, "Factors in Achieving Victory in Future Military Conflicts."

41   "Meeting of Defense Ministry Board," National Defense Control Center.

42   Some Russian leaders also believe that the United States is a country in economic, diplomatic, military, and social decline because of domestic polarization and other factors. Chinese leaders have made similar statements. These two arguments—that the United States will remain Moscow's main enemy and is a declining power—are in conflict. Nevertheless, Russian military thinking still centers on the United States as the main threat. For a broad overview of this thinking, see, for example, Andrei Martyanov, *Disintegration: Indicators of the Coming American Collapse* (Atlanta, GA: Clarity Press, 2021).

43   Khomutov, "Countering the 'Multi-Domain Operations' of the Adversary."

44   U.S. Marine Corps, Force Design 2030 (Washington, DC: Department of the Navy, March 2020), 2, https://www.marines.mil/Force-Design-2030/.

45   Ibid.

46   Author interviews with Ukrainian, U.S., and European officials, June 2023.

47   И. Л. Макарчук, К. А. Троценко [I.L. Makarchuk and K.A. Trotsenko], "Характер Операций Современных Армий. Мультиразумные Сетевые Военные Системы И Тактика Их Действий" [The Nature of Operations of Modern Armies: Multi-Intelligence Networked Military Systems and Their Tactics], Военная мысль [*Military Thought*] 32, no. 1 (March 2023): 65-84.

48   Lester Grau and Charles K. Bartles, *The Russian Way of War: Force Structure, Tactics, and Modernization of the Russian Ground Forces* (Fort Leavenworth, KS: Foreign Military Studies Office, 2016), 27-28, https://www.armyupress.army.mil/portals/7/hot%20spots/documents/russia/2017-07-the-russian-way-of-war-grau-bartles.pdf; and Mike Eckel, "Russia Proposes Major Military Reorganization, Conscription Changes, Increase in Troop Numbers," Radio Free Europe / Radio Liberty, December 23, 2022, https://www.rferl.org/a/russia-military-reorganization-expansion/32190811.html.

49   "Meeting of Defense Ministry Board," National Defense Control Center; "Russia's defense chief proposes re-establishing Moscow, Leningrad military districts," TASS, December 21, 2022, https://tass.com/defense/1554071; Valius Venckunas, "Nine New Aviation Regiments to Be Created in Major Russian Army Restructuring," Ministry of Defence of the Russian Federation, December 12, 2022; and Eckel, "Russia Proposes Major Military Reorganization."

50   "Meeting of Defense Ministry Board," National Defense Control Center; "Russia's defense chief proposes re-establishing Moscow, Leningrad military districts," TASS; and Eckel, "Russia Proposes Major Military Reorganization."

51   Grau and Bartles, *The Russian Way of War*, 27-8.

52   "Meeting of Defense Ministry Board," National Defense Control Center.

53   For Russian combat training, see Main Directorate of Combat Training of the Armed Forces of the Russian Federation, Особенности ведения боевых действий в городе (населенном пункте) и лесозащитной полосе в составе штурмового отряда (роты, взвода) [*Features of Conducting Combat Operations in a City (Settlement) and a Forest Protection Zone as Part of an Assault Detachment (Company, Platoon)*] (Moscow: Ministry

Of Defence, 2022), https://m.censor.net/ru/news/3386414/minoborony_rossii_izdalo_metodichku_po_shturmovym_deyistviyam_po_opytu_voyiny_protiv_ukrainy_dokument. On Russian operations in Ukraine, also see Michael Kofman and Rob Lee, "Perseverance and Adaptation: Ukraine's Counteroffensive at Three Months," War on the Rocks, September 4, 2023, https://warontherocks.com/2023/09/perseverance-and-adaptation-ukraines-counteroffensive-at-three-months/.

54 This information is based on a range of Russian manuals captured by Ukrainian forces in Ukraine. There is also a rich tradition in Russian and Soviet doctrine for assault units. See, for example Grau and Bartles, *The Russian Way of War*.

55 Author interviews with Ukrainian, U.S., and European officials, June 2023. Also see Jack Watling and Nick Reynolds, *Meatgrinder: Russian Tactics in the Second Year of Its Invasion of Ukraine* (London: Royal United Services Institute, May 19, 2023).

56 See, for example, А. А. Плужников, О. Б. Усачёв [A.A. Pluzhnikov and O.B. Usachev], "Современные Требования К Общевойсковым Формированиям Тактического Звена" [Current Requirements for Tactical-Level Combined Arms Formations], Военная мысль [*Military Thought*] 31, no. 4 (Month/Year): 41–56; and Makarchuk and Trotsenko, Характер "The Nature of Operations of Modern Armies: Overdue Change."

57 "Шойгу Поручил Усилить Боевую Составляющую ВМФ, ВКС и РВСН" [Shoigu instructed to strengthen the combat component of the Navy, Aerospace Forces and Strategic Missile Forces], TASS, January 17, 2022, https://tass.ru/armiya-i-opk/16814813.

58 Makarchuk and Trotsenko, "The Nature of Operations of Modern Armies: Multi-Intelligence Networked Military Systems and Their Tactics."

59 Makarchuk and Trotsenko, "The Nature of Operations of Modern Armies: Overdue Change."

60 Makarchuk and Trotsenko, "The Nature of Operations of Modern Armies: Multi-Intelligence Networked Military Systems and Their Tactics."

61 Ibid.

62 Makarchuk and Trotsenko, "The Nature of Operations of Modern Armies: Overdue Change."

63 Ibid.

64 Makarchuk and Trotsenko, "The Nature of Operations of Modern Armies: Multi-Intelligence Networked Military Systems and Their Tactics," 80.

65 On the role of non-state and quasi-state actors see, for example, Makarchuk and Trotsenko, "The Nature of Operations of Modern Armies: Overdue Change"; И. Л. Макарчук, К. А. Троценко [I.L. Makarchuk and K.A. Trotsenko], "Характер Операций Современных Армий. Уроки И Выводы По Итогам Войны В Афганистане (2001-2021 гг.)" [The Nature of Operations of Modern Armies: Lessons and Conclusions from the War in Afghanistan (2001-2021)], Военная мысль [*Military Thought*] 32, no. 1 (March 2023): 48–64; and Makarchuk and Trotsenko, "The Nature of Operations of Modern Armies: Multi-Intelligence Networked Military Systems and Their Tactics."

66 See, for example, А. А. Цыганов, М. М. Дебело, С. В. Бандура [A.A. Tsyganov, M.M. Debelo, and S.V. Bandura], "О Необходимости Создания Перспективных Объединений Воздушно-космических Сил Для Прикрытия Объектов Высших Звеньев Управления И Стратегических Ядерных Сил" [The Need for Prospective Large Commands of Aerospace Forces for Point Air Defense of Top Command Levels and Strategic Nuclear Forces], Военная мысль [*Military Thought*] 32, no. 1 (March 2023): 31–38.

67 "Meeting of Defense Ministry Board," National Defense Control Center.

68 Ibid.

69 Valius Venckunas, "Nine New Aviation Regiments to Be Created in Major Russian Army Restructuring," Ministry of Defense of the Russian Federation, December 12, 2022; and "Russia's defense chief proposes re-establishing Moscow, Leningrad military districts," TASS.

70 Yermolin, Zubov, and Fomin, "Use of Aerospace Forces' Strike Aviation in Future Military Conflicts."

71 Mohammad, Pokhvashchev, and Ryazantsev, "Improving the Efficiency of Countering Small Unmanned Aerial Vehicles"; and Kogtin and Shaidurov, "Development Prospects for Small Unmanned Aerial."

72 Ulanov, "Forecast of Trends."

73 А. В. Топоров, М. С. Бондарь, Р. В. Ахметьянов [A.V. Toporov, M.S. Bondar, and R.V. Akhmetyanov], "Материально-техническая Поддержка В Бою И Операции: Проблемный Вопрос И Направления Его Разрешения" [Logistical Support in Combat and Operations: A Problem and Potential Solutions], Военная мысль [*Military Thought*] 32, no. 2 (June 2023): 17-31.

74 Yermolin, Zubov, and Fomin, "Use of Aerospace Forces' Strike Aviation in Future Military Conflicts."

75 Ibid.

76 "Russia tests engine for next-generation strategic missile-carrying bomber," TASS, October 31, 2022, https://tass.com/defense/1529991.

77 "Russia's second Tu-160M strategic bomber sent to flight tests - source," TASS, February 17, 2023, https://tass.com/russia/1578231.

78 А. В. Николаев [A.V. Nikolayev], "Перспективы Применения Авиационного Артиллерийского Оружия На Самолетах Шестого Поколения" [Prospects of Using Aviation Artillery Weapons on Sixth-Generation Aircraft], Военная мысль [*Military Thought*] 32, no. 2 (June 2023): 147-56.

79 "Meeting of Defense Ministry Board," National Defense Control Center.

80 Russian Federation, *Maritime Doctrine of the Russian Federation* (Moscow: Kremlin, July 2022), translated by Anna Davis and Ryan Vest, U.S. Naval War College, https://dnnlgwick.blob.core.windows.net/portals/0/NWCDepartments/Russia%20Maritime%20Studies%20Institute/20220731_ENG_RUS_Maritime_Doctrine_FINALtxt.pdf?sv=2017-04-17&sr=b&si=DNNFileManagerPolicy&sig=2zUFSaTUSPcOpQDBk%2FuCtVnb%2FDoy06Cbh0EI5tGpl2Y%3D.

81 "Meeting of Defense Ministry Board," National Defense Control Center.

82 Ulanov, "Forecast of Trends," 102.

83 Kari A. Bingen, Kaitlyn Johnson, and Makena Young, *Space Threat Assessment 2023* (Washington, DC: CSIS, April 2023), 14-15, https://www.csis.org/analysis/space-threat-assessment-2023.

84 See, for example, Ramin Skibba, "Russia's Space Program Is in Big Trouble," Wired, March 20, 2023, https://www.wired.com/story/russias-space-program-is-in-big-trouble/.

85 Microsoft, *An overview of Russia's cyberattack activity in Ukraine* (Redmond, WA: Digital

Security Unit, Microsoft, April 2022), https://query.prod.cms.rt.microsoft.com/cms/api/am/binary/RE4Vwwd.

86 Kharchenko and Kalutsky, "Assessing the Contribution of an Electronic Warfare Grouping to the Reduction of Enemy Combat Capabilities"; Galkin, Dyatlov, and Stepanov, "Advanced Military Applied Technologies"; and Lopin, Smirnov, and Tkachov, "Development of Assets to Counter Unmanned Vehicles."

87 "Meeting of Defense Ministry Board," National Defense Control Center; "Russia's defense chief proposes re-establishing Moscow, Leningrad military districts," TASS; Valius Venckunas, "Nine New Aviation Regiments to Be Created in Major Russian Army Restructuring," Ministry of Defence of the Russian Federation, December 12, 2022; and Eckel, "Russia Proposes Major Military Reorganization."

88 "Russia Plans Huge Defence Spending Hike in 2024 as War Drags," *Bloomberg*, September 22, 2023, https://www.bloomberg.com/news/articles/2023-09-22/russia-plans-huge-defense-spending-hike-in-2024-as-war-drags-on?embedded-checkout=true.

89 Mike Plunkett, "Unchartered Waters: Russian Naval Shipbuilding Moves to Navigate Sanctions," Janes Navy International, July 28, 2023

90 Jack Watling and Nick Reynolds, Stormbreak: Fighting Through Russian Defences in Ukraine's 2023 Offensive (London: Royal United Services Institute for Defence and Security Studies, September 2023), https://www.rusi.org/explore-our-research/publications/special-resources/stormbreak-fighting-through-russian-defences-ukraines-2023-offensive.

Chapter 4: Conclusion

1 Константин Сивков [Konstantin Sivkov], "Украина—только начало: Геополитическим последствием спецоперации станет изменение" [Ukraine Is Just the Beginning: The Geopolitical Consequences of the Special Operation Will Change the Entire View of the World], Военно-промышленный курьер [*Military-Industrial Courier*], March 28, 2022; and В. Б. Зарудницкий [Z.B. Zarudnitsky], "Факторы Достижения Победы В Военных Конфликтах Будущего" [Factors in Achieving Victory in Future Military Conflicts], Военная мысль [*Military Thought*] 30, no. 1 (2021): 39-54.

2 "Meeting of Defense Ministry Board," National Defense Control Center, Moscow, December 21, 2022, http://en.kremlin.ru/events/president/transcripts/70159.

3 "US became party to Ukraine conflict long ago with goal of destroying Russia - diplomat," TASS, May 4, 2023, https://tass.com/politics/1613855.

4 On Russian perceptions see, for example, "Meeting of Defense Ministry Board," National Defense Control Center. As one article noted about the United States and Ukraine, "The regime in our neighboring country is completely under American political influence and has consequently become a tool for fighting Russia. Consequently, Russia's special military operation is also a counteraction to US attempts to preserve the existing world order led by Western and American leadership." И.А. Копылов, В.В. Толстых [I.A. Kopylov and V.V. Tolstykh], "Оценка влияния политического фактора на управление национальной обороной Российской Федерации" [Assessing the Impact of the Political Factor on Russia's National Defense Management], Военная мысль [*Military Thought*] 32, no. 1 (2023), 3.

5 NATO, "Madrid Summit Declaration," press release, June 29, 2022, https://www.nato.int/cps/en/natohq/official_texts_196951.htm.

6 The data in the table come from G.F. Krivosheev, ed., *Soviet Casualties and Combat Losses in the Twentieth Century* (Mechanicsburg, PA: Stackpole Books, 1997), 281-90; D.S. Ryabushkin,

"Mify Damanskogo" [Myths of Damansky] (Russia: AST, 2004), 151, 263-64, https://coollib.com/b/368428-dmitriy-sergeevich-ryabushkin-mifyi-damanskogo/read; "Nekotoryye maloizvestnyye epizody pogranichnogo konflikta na o. Damanskom" [Some Little-Known Episodes of the Border Conflict on Damansky Island], Voyennoye oruzhiye i armii Mira [Military Weapons and Armies of the World], accessed February 14, 2023, https://warfor.me/nekotoryie-maloizvestnyie-epizodyi-pogranichnogo-konflikta-na-o-damanskom/; Lester Grau and Michael A. Gress, eds., *The Soviet -Afghan War: How a Superpower Fought and Lost* (Lawrence, KS: University of Kansas Press, 2022); Lester W. Grau, *The Bear Went Over the Mountain: Soviet Combat Tactics in Afghanistan* (New York: Frank Cass, 1998), xiv; John B. Dunlop, "How Many Soldiers and Civilians Died During the Russo-Chechen War of 1994-1996?," *Central Asia Survey* 19, no. 3/4 (2000): 329-39; Simon Saradzhyan, "Army Learned few Lessons from Chechnya," *Moscow Times*, March 9, 2005; Mark Galeotti, *The Modern Russian Army 1992-2016* (New York: Osprey, 2017); Robyn Dixon, Sudarasan Raghavan, Isabelle Khurshudyan, and David L. Stern, "Russia's War Dead Belie Its Slogan That No One Is Left Behind," *Washington Post*, April 8, 2022, https://www.washingtonpost.com/world/2022/04/08/russia-war-dead-soldiers-bodies/; Abdullaev, "Death Toll Put at 160,000 in Chechnya"; "Russia Lost 64 Troops in Georgia War, 283 Wounded," Reuters, February 21, 2009, https://www.reuters.com/article/us-russia-georgia-deaths/russia-lost-64-troops-in-georgia-war-283-wounded-idUKTRE51K1B820090221; "Nearly 585,000 People Have Been Killed Since the Beginning of the Syrian Revolution," Syrian Observatory for Human Rights, January 4, 2020, https://www.syriahr.com/en/152189/; "Conflict-Related Civilian Casualties in Ukraine," United Nations Human Rights, Office of the High Commissioner, January 27, 2022, https://ukraine.un.org/sites/default/files/2022-02/Conflict-related%20civilian%20casualties%20as%20of%2031%20December%202021%20%28rev%2027%20January%202022%29%20corr%20EN_0.pdf; Ministry of Defence, Twitter post, February 17, 2023, 1:45 a.m.; "The Total Combat Losses of the Enemy from 24.02.22 to 18.02.23," Ministry of Defence of Ukraine, February 28, 2023, https://www.mil.gov.ua/en/news/2023/02/18/the-total-combat-losses-of-the-enemy-from-24-02-22-to-18-02-23/; Helene Cooper, Eric Schmitt, and Thomas Gibbons-Neff, "Soaring Death Toll Gives Grim Insight Into Russian Tactics," *New York Times*, February 2, 2023, https://www.nytimes.com/2023/02/02/us/politics/ukraine-russia-casualties.html; ОльгаИвшина [Olga Ivshina], "Впять раз больше, чем обычно: что известно о потерях России в Украине к середине февраля" [Five Times More Than Usual: What Is Known about the Losses of Russia in Ukraine by Mid-February], BBC, February 17, 2023, https://www.bbc.com/russian/features-64680032; and authors' estimates and interviews with U.S. and other Western officials, 2023.

7   "Meeting of Defense Ministry Board," National Defense Control Center.

8   Zoltan Barany, "Armies and Autocrats: Why Putin's Military Failed," *Journal of Democracy* 34, no. 1 (January 2023): 80-94, https://www.journalofdemocracy.org/articles/armies-and-autocrats-why-putins-military-failed.

9   Chelsey Dulaney, "Russia's Ruble Slides on Capital-Flight Fears," *Wall Street Journal*, April 6, 2023, https://www.wsj.com/articles/russias-ruble-slides-on-capital-flight-fears-9d86273e.

10 "Transcript of April 2023 World Economic Outlook Press Briefing," International Monetary Fund, April 11, 2023, https://www.imf.org/en/News/Articles/2023/04/12/tr41123-weo-press-briefing-transcript.

11 Vasily Zatsepin and Vitaly Tsymbal, "Military Economy and Military Reform in Russia," in Alexander Abramov et al., *Russian Economy in 2017: Trends and Outlooks* (Moscow: Gaidar Institute, 2018), 515-25, https://www.iep.ru/en/publications/publication/8343.html.

12 See, for example, Lester Grau and Charles K. Bartles, *The Russian Way of War: Force*

Structure, Tactics, and Modernization of the Russian Ground Forces (Fort Leavenworth, KS: Foreign Military Studies Office, 2016), https://www.armyupress.army.mil/portals/7/hot%20 spots/documents/russia/2017-07-the-russian-way-of-war-grau-bartles.pdf.

13 See, for example, Josie Stewart and Joseph Moore, "Can Ukraine Thank Russian Corruption for Hindering Their Invasion?," Transparency International, March 1, 2023, https://ti-defence.org/can-ukraine-thank-russian-corruption-for-hindering-their-invasion/.

14 Author interviews U.S. and European officials, June 2023. Also see such secondary sources as Michael Kofman and Rob Lee, "Perseverance and Adaptation: Ukraine's Counteroffensive at Three Months," War on the Rocks, September 4, 2023, https://warontherocks.com/2023/09/perseverance-and-adaptation-ukraines-counteroffensive-at-three-months/; and Paul D. Shinkman, "How Russian Corruption Is Foiling Putin's Army in Ukraine," *U.S. News and World Report*, August 31, 2022, https://www.usnews.com/news/world-report/articles/2022-08-31/how-russian-corruption-is-foiling-putins-army-in-ukraine.

15 Barany, "Armies and Autocrats."

16 Andrei V Kozyrev (@andreivkosyrev), Twitter post, March 6, 2022, 3:16 p.m., https://twitter.com/andreivkozyrev/status/1500611398245634050.

17 John Chipman, "John Chipman's Military Balance Launch Event Remarks," International Institute of Strategic Studies, February 15, 2023, https://www.iiss.org/blogs/analysis/2023/02/john-chipmansmilitary-balance-launch-event-remarks.

18 Max Bergmann et al., *Out of Stock? Assessing the Impact of Sanctions on Russia's Defense Industry* (Washington, DC: CSIS), https://www.csis.org/analysis/out-stock-assessing-impact-sanctions-russias-defense-industry.

19 Russian Federation, *Maritime Doctrine of the Russian Federation* (Moscow: Kremlin, July 2022), https://dnnlgwick.blob.core.windows.net/portals/0/NWCDepartments/Russia%20Maritime%20Studies%20Institute/20220731_ENG_RUS_Maritime_Doctrine_FINALtxt.pdf?sv=2017-04-17&sr=b&si=DNNFileManagerPolicy&sig=2zUFSaTUSPcOpQDBk%2FuCtVnb%2FDoy06CbhOEI5tGpl2Y%3D.

20 Barany, "Armies and Autocrats."

21 Samuel P. Huntington, *The Soldier and the State: The Theory and Politics of Civil-Military Relations* (Cambridge, MA: Harvard University Press, 1957), 2.

22 Александр Андреевич Свечин [Alexander Andreyevich Svechin], Стратегия [*Strategy*] (Moscow: Gosvoenizdat, 1926), 8.